# Inglo

CW00818727

# Revolution

*How membership of the European Union has subverted the English Constitution and how we are now living in an illegally constituted state.*

## Gerard Batten MEP
## &
## Pavel Stroilov

*"...will assist and defend all Jurisdictions, Pre-eminences, and Authorities, granted to Her Majesty, and annexed to the Crown by Acts of Parliament, or otherwise, against all Foreign Princes, Persons, Prelates, States, or Potentates".*
(Current Privy Council Oath of Allegiance)

*"Our sovereignty has been taken away by the European Court of Justice...no longer is European law an incoming tide flowing up the estuaries of England. It is now like tidal wave bringing down our sea walls and flowing inland over our fields and houses – to the dismay of all".*
(Lord Denning, Master of the Rolls. Bruges Group 1990).

*"Does Magna Carta mean nothing to you?*
*Did she die in vain?"*
(Tony Hancock. 1959)

First Published 2013
Text Copyright © Gerard Batten MEP & Pavel Stroilov 2013
Gerard Batten MEP & Pavel Stroilov assert their moral rights to be regarded as the authors of this book.
info@BretwaldaBooks.com
www.BretwaldaBooks.com
ISBN 978-1-909099-77-7
Illustrations courtesy of the publisher except: Cover Mgimelfarb; p88 World Economic Forum; p74 Allan warren

# CONTENTS

# Foreword

Since becoming an MEP in 2004 I felt the need to write something on the illegality of Britain's membership of the European Union under the English Constitution. A couple of years ago I read Albert Burgess' concise and excellent booklet entitled, 'A Layman's Guide to the English Constitution'. This inspired me to revisit the subject, but lack of time prevented me from doing the extensive research required.

At that point my brilliant research assistant and friend, Pavel Stroilov entered the picture. I mapped out the territory to be covered and asked Pavel to begin. With his usual determination and intellectual rigour Pavel had soon expanded the scope of the project. This book would not have been possible without Pavel's assistance, and it is very much the product of his excellent research.

It is illustrative of the times we live in that those charged with protecting our freedoms, the elected politicians, the courts and the lawyers, seem most ignorant of the existence, origin and purpose of those freedoms under our law. It has taken a young Russian refugee from a despotic regime to explain clearly how the freedoms under which we used to live have been betrayed, set aside, and subverted by those whose duty it is to protect them. In the words of our mutual friend the heroic Soviet dissident, Vladimir Bukovsky, "I have lived in your future and it doesn't work."

It is for our country to decide what to do with the priceless heritage left to us by our ancestors. If the people choose to bury the ancient English Constitution and live in an illegally constituted, clapped-out, undemocratic Region of a United States of Europe - in fact if not yet in name – that is their choice. But any genuine choice should be based on knowledge. The story of English history is no longer taught in schools, still less the evolution of our laws, Constitution, and customs.

In this book, we endeavour to redress the balance a little and to prove (within the limits of time and space available to us):

1. That the most fundamental principles of the English Common Law Constitution, such as the Rule of Law, Sovereignty, or Government by Consent, cannot be abolished or altered by statute or any other legal means;

2. That the actions of successive Tory and Labour governments in the past forty years, especially through the 'transfer of sovereignty' to the European Union, have unlawfully set aside all those principles;

3. That those actions were thus illegal under the English Constitution and, therefore, void in law;

4. That those anti-constitutional actions can and must be legally reversed, and the Constitution restored.

Just before this book went to press Prime Minister David Cameron made a long awaited speech on Britain and the European Union. In a nutshell, Mr Cameron promised a referendum on the EU, provided of course that the electorate return a Conservative Government in 2015. He seeks a mandate to 'renegotiate', and promises a new 'settlement' with the EU 'with the Single Market at its heart', and that his renegotiated terms will be put to an 'in or out' referendum by 2018. But Mr Cameron does not want Britain to leave the European Union. He refuses to be drawn on his position if he fails to obtain the renegotiated terms he wants – and he has yet to say exactly what those terms will be.

What Mr Cameron proposes is in fact a re-run of what Harold Wilson did in 1974-1975, except that this time it will be in slow-motion. Harold Wilson secured a Labour victory in the 1974 General Election on the same promise of renegotiated terms. He secured a few minor cosmetic concessions from the then EEC, and campaigned for a 'Yes' vote in the 1975 referendum. Just as Harold Wilson put the fiction of the Common Market at the forefront of his campaign in 1975, so David Cameron intends to put the fiction of the Single Market at the forefront of his, if indeed the referendum ever happens.

There is no guarantee that the EU will play ball again this time. Any return of powers from the EU to the nation state requires a new Treaty with the unanimous agreement of all Member States - in the EU it takes 27 (soon to be 28) to tango. The other member states are not going to agree to special and less onerous terms of membership for Britain. The cause of Mr Cameron's speech was not any genuine desire to mitigate the detrimental effects of EU membership on Britain. It was a desperate response to the political threat from UKIP.

UKIP has used the blunt, but effective, weapon of taking votes at the ballot box. It may not have won seats at Westminster yet while it has deprived other parties of votes and changed the outcome of elections. Governments do not care about public opinion or petitions, what they care about are votes: gaining them and losing them. After 20 years of relentless work UKIP has put the issue of EU membership back on the political agenda by using the democratic process.

There is of course no need for Mr Cameron to go through the elaborate process he proposes over the next five years. He could, with Parliament's approval, hold an in-or-out referendum within months. The issues now are the same as they were in 1975. We gain no real economic or material benefits from EU membership, and even if we did they would not be worth the loss of democratic control over our own affairs.

The proposition of this book is not party political as such. It is about our Constitution; our tried and tested laws and liberties; and our right to live and be governed according to those ancient laws and customs. The contents may not be political but the solutions inescapably are. Unless our ill-advised Sovereign and her Ministers recognise their errors and rectify them then there is no alternative but for a political fight by those who still believe in the English Constitution.

In 1688 a rebellion ended the despotic rule of James II and brought about the Glorious Revolution that created the constitutional settlement under which we lived until 1973. That settlement was betrayed and overthrown by a process of lies, deceit and treason that can in contrast be described as an Inglorious Revolution.

It may be the destiny of the English to end their long and honourable history as vassals of a great new undemocratic European empire; but every true English man and woman has the right to resist - if they choose to do so.

# Part I. Constitution

**BRITAIN DOES HAVE A WRITTEN CONSTITUTION**

Just a hundred years ago, and for centuries before that, it was a fashion of all British statesmen to swear their oaths by the Constitution, to make threats and promises in the name of the Constitution, to curse their opponents as enemies of the Constitution. That Constitution was cherished as the greatest achievement in the history of statehood. It was imitated, successfully or not, by our foreign friends and foes over five continents. No other concept stood higher in this country's political scale of values; and even if nothing else was stable, the great English Constitution remained immutable.

Yet hardly more than a faint memory of it has survived to this day. Few people nowadays are certain what the Constitution is, and many even doubt that it exists. Indeed, one will often hear today that Britain has no constitution, or at least, no written constitution. As if that was an omission which needs to be rectified. As if what is commonly called a 'written constitution' is a necessary landmark in the political progress of any civilized nation - and we barbarians are now several centuries behind in achieving it.

The absurdity of this idea is such that it could hardly result from mere ignorance, but only from a concerted effort of propaganda. Even the superficial factual premise is false: the British Constitution is not 'unwritten'. Far from that, it is written many times over: we find essentially the same provisions in Magna Carta, in the Bill of Rights, in all other Constitutional Acts, in the landmark judgements of our courts ruling on constitutional cases, etc.

More to the point is the fact that the very idea of a Constitution in its modern form (meaning, roughly, the law on how the nation is governed) is British in origin. Nearly all 'written' constitutions in the past three centuries have been imitations of the British 'unwritten' one. Obvious and recent examples are all constitutions in the Commonwealth; but there are more. The US Constitution purported to re-assert the principles of the British Constitution against what was seen as the arbitrary and unconstitutional actions of the Crown.

Many constitutions in Europe were consciously copied from our 'unwritten' constitution. Others found their origins in the ideas of the French Revolution; and the idea was to replace the 'unreasonable' French autocracy with something akin to the 'reasonable' English Constitution (or, rather, such a poor understanding of it as the French revolutionaries had). Virtually all democratic constitutions over the world find their origin, directly or indirectly, in the English constitution.

It is a different matter that most of them have been rather poor imitations. Our constitution is a very advanced system, whose delicate balances are not easy to copy. More often than not, reducing our complex system of principles, precedents, rules and conventions to a single written code was precisely where such attempts at imitation would go amiss. But even such nations who failed to import our constitutional machinery have accepted our constitutional ideals of Democracy, Liberty, and Rule of Law. All those things, in their modern form, had been developed in the English common law. Those things are easily declared, easily taken for granted, and easily lost. But they were not easy to develop in practice, and they were not brought to this world by Martians. They were brought by the English.

This simple fact of history is only too readily forgotten by the political class who care nothing for the heritage of our country and even less for the future of democracy. It is forgotten that for the most part, the history of civilisation has been a history of despotism, with democracies as happy but rare exceptions, with England by far the most notable exception. It is forgotten how often the ideals of liberty have been pursued, yet how rarely attained; how easy it is to put rights into a declaration, and how difficult to put them into practice. England is one country which has successfully put all these things into practice.

By trial and error, century after century, we have developed this unique political system called freedom under the law. Better constitutions may have existed on paper; but so far, no better constitution has ever existed in practice. England was the nation that proved that freedom under the law was even possible; only then did it begin to spread around the world. Alas, it has not conquered the world and it is disappearing from England.

So the great debate about our sovereignty, which should have been at the forefront of our political life, but is instead vehemently suppressed – that debate has a wider international significance. Nothing can be more dishonest than to ridicule the concerns at the destruction of our constitution as Little England's nostalgia for an outdated legal fiction. Our sovereignty stands for the English Constitution, and the English Constitution stands for freedom under the law.

In the modern context, if the word 'democracy' means anything at all, it means a Constitution like the English one. The phrase 'rule of law', when it means anything at all, means a Constitution like the English one. When we are told that a nation in a remote corner of the world is in revolt against dictatorship, if this is true, this means they aspire to a Constitution like the English one. When we are told to replace our ancient 'unwritten' constitution with a modern 'written' one, what this really means is that we should have democracy on paper, but not in practice. When we are told that our national sovereignty has outlived its time and should give way to the "pooling of sovereignty". That theory has only one real meaning: that freedom under the law should be sacrificed in the interests of some anti-democratic Utopian ideal.

### THE COMMON LAW CONSTITUTION

The English law in general, and the English Constitution in particular, were never 'granted' from above. They grew from below. It is manifestly untrue that we have no legal codes or declarations of the kind which some other nations chose to headline as 'Constitutions'. But it is, fortunately, true that we have had no great law-givers like Moses, Solon, or Napoleon. Our Constitution is not unwritten; but it is anonymous. All the great names in our legal history belong not to legislators, but to judges such as Bracton or Coke; celebrated for keeping the law as it was, and emphatically not for making any new ones.

The beginnings of the Common Law are found not in any legislation, but in customs observed for so long that (as the legal phrase used to be) "the memory of men runneth not to the contrary". In the words of Sir Alfred Denning (as he then was): *"the law of England was in former times for the most part declared by the judges, who were guided by the precedents of their predecessors. They decided each case as justice demanded and then built up principles from the individual cases. The precedents were collected and reported, and form a body of case-law unique in the history of the world". (Sir Alfred Denning. The Changing law. London, 1953, p. 5)*

The origins of our most ancient laws are thus lost to memory, and for most purposes, it does not matter whether (as different lawyers in different ages suggested) they were found in the law of God, the common sense of the populace, or forgotten statutes of some ancient kings; be that as it may, those customs were recognised as law for their very antiquity. Once recognised, they had to be consistently applied to great and small controversies arising in the changing world. Once they were so applied, that precedent also became binding in law. So the judges, conscious of their responsibility as law-givers as well as law-finders, had to formulate the law with utmost care and precision.

So the English justice system accumulates the experience, wisdom and diligence of countless generations, while continental justice relies on the experience, wisdom and diligence of a particular legislator. The continental laws are based on someone's ideas - which may be good or bad. The English law is based on real life.

The continental laws are naturally political and English Common law is not. The continental laws are inevitably affected by the prejudices of the age when they were made, and have to be changed every now and then to reflect newer prejudices. The English law is flexible enough to be immutable and eternal. Consequently to all that, a continental judge is little more than a bureaucrat, while an English judge is little less than a King Solomon - in the magnitude of his duty if not his wisdom.

Any continental 'written' Constitution would normally begin with a statement of some political ideals which are declared to be the ultimate goal of human existence, for example 'Liberty, Equality and Fraternity', or 'ever closer union between the peoples of Europe'. Then come separate headings of what the state should do to achieve that, for example, organise elections, raise taxes, create a central bank and a currency, guarantee human rights, maintain an army, set up a judicial system, regulate economy, etc., etc. Then, under each of these headings, come detailed laws on how exactly each of those things may or should be done and what are the rights and obligations of each interested party.

Eventually, every paragraph should be interpreted with reference to the general political declarations of its goals. As a result, the law, and especially the constitutional law, is begotten in the politics of the time, and necessarily changes with time. People and especially politicians may well lose their faith in liberty, equality and fraternity and then believe in a Fuhrer, fatherland, or Socialism. On the other hand, the interpretation of those ideals may also change dramatically. They are not stable because they are dependent on the politics of the day.

By contrast, the English Constitution is emphatically neutral, even blind, towards politics. Instead, it rests upon purely legal principles: Rule of Law, Freedom under the Law, Government by Consent, Sovereignty; derived not from political declarations, but from the practical justice of the Common Law. The names of these principles are much newer than their origins. The consistent application of those principles to the multitude of practical controversies has filled them with real meaning. The core of our Constitution was forged by the Common Law blacksmiths. It was only after it had worked in practice for many centuries that solemn declarations followed. Our celebrated constitutional statutes, such as Magna Carta or the Bill of Rights, merely re-stated the Common Law long recognised as the law of times immemorial.

Similar words were used and similar liberties proclaimed in many continental declarations; but without the rich and definite substance provided by the Common Law, they remained mere declarations. The French Revolution produced a well-written Declaration of the Rights of Man and the Citizen one day, and then began the tremendous bloodbath of mass terror the next day. Germany adopted the excellently democratic Weimar Constitution which endured no longer than until the general election that saw the victory of the Nazis.

This is how, while continental thinkers constantly dreamt about eternal and impersonal justice, we were the nation who found a way to put it into practice. Century after century, we went through millions of controversies presented by the real life, and endeavoured, as best we could, to resolve them both justly and consistently with the principle and the precedent. So, by trial and error, we have succeeded where great continental prophets failed. In the maze of political realities, in the fog of political theories, we have found the right path to freedom under the law.

### THE RULE OF LAW

The continental tradition treats the word 'law' as synonymous with 'legislation'. The common law tradition treats the same word as synonymous with 'liberties'. In this fundamental sense, English law and continental law are not merely different, but direct opposites.

Europe prides itself at tracing the origins of its legal tradition to Ancient Rome; and in fairness, there is much in that heritage to be proud about. But the constitutional basis of it is the famous maxim of Justinian: *Quod principi placuit legis habet vigorem* - 'whatever pleases the Prince has the force of law' (Institutes 1.2.6). Their law, with all its virtues, remains a creature of the state and may be changed or abolished by the state.

The basis of our constitution is the very opposite of Justinian's. Symbolically, our constitutional credo has been formulated by a great common law judge rather than a great king or emperor, when in the 13th century Chief Justice Bracton declared: *Rex non debet esse sub homine, sed sub Deo et sub lege, quia lex facit regem* - 'the King can be under no man, but under the God and Law; for it is Law that makes the King'.

Such is the basic constitutional dilemma faced by every society: to be governed by the rules or by the rulers. Those are the only two conceivable bases of government, and no third way has ever been invented. The dilemma is as ancient as the very ideas of law and state. Consider, for example, the Biblical description of Ancient Israel being governed only by the Law (and the Judges administering it): *"In those days there was no king in Israel: every man did that which was right in his own eyes."* The people then demand to have a king, so "that we also may be like all the nations". God obviously dislikes the idea, a prophet protests vociferously that people's liberty and property will no longer be safe; but the people defy all reason, and God reluctantly chooses as good a king for them as you could wish for. Sure enough, his reign ends most unhappily in tyranny and civil war. Sir John Fortesque refers to the Book of Kings to explain the peculiarity of English Constitution in De Laudibus Legum Anglie, c. IX (In praise of the laws of England).

Of course, there is something to say, and a lot has been said, on both sides of that eternal argument. All we need to know for the present purposes is that England has made that choice, and enshrined its preference in the Constitution under the name of the Rule of Law. Of course, our system does allow for a limited government, just like the alternative system allows for limited law. The point is that, in our system, the law comes first. Ultimately, ours is a nation governed by rules, not by rulers; by right, and not might; it is not the state that makes the law – it is the law that makes the state. Where there is a dispute between the sovereign and a subject, the law treats them equally, like any other two parties in a legal dispute. There is no presumption that the government is lawful. There is no presumption that a rebellion is unlawful. Both must be judged on their merits.

Nowadays, after centuries of testing both systems in practice, nearly every constitution in the world declares the principle of the rule of law. But it was not always so; and even today, what they mean by rule of law is not the same as what it means in the English Constitution. The whole point of the Common Law is that a principle, once declared to be law, has to be consistently applied to every practical controversy; and from that, the whole body of law grows. The famous marvels of the common law grew up as logical extensions or practical safeguards of that principle: the sacred rights of liberty and property, trial by jury, habeas corpus, 'innocent until proven guilty', punishment to match the offence, prohibition of cruel or unusual punishment, the right of access to justice, etc.

Thus, individual freedom and limited government were always inherent in the rule of law. The individual is free to do anything unless it is expressly prohibited by law; and the government (indeed, any 'public authority') is forbidden to do anything unless it is expressly authorised by law.

To enforce the latter principle, the Common Law developed a system of 'prerogative writs' whereby the lawfulness of any government activity may be challenged and remedied in court. Any unlawful decision of any 'public authority' can be quashed by a writ of *Certiorari* (Quashing Order), any unlawful practice prohibited by a writ of *Prohibitio* (Prohibiting Order), and the authority can be compelled to do its legal duty by a writ of *Mandamus* (Mandating Order). Those three ancient 'writs', now re-named 'orders', and incorporated in the procedure of 'judicial review'. But the most ancient, important and famous of all prerogative writs remains elevated above the ordinary procedure, as it has always been; for it protects the liberty of the subject. That is, of course, the writ of Habeas Corpus (Produce the Body).

Habeas Corpus dates back at least to Magna Carta, and probably earlier. The Habeas Corpus Act 1679, sometimes mistakenly credited for creating the system, merely introduced a few additional procedural safeguards. The legal tradition links it with the famous C. 39 of Magna Carta: "No freeman shall be taken or imprisoned or disseised (wrongfully deprived) or exiled or in any way destroyed, nor will we go upon him nor send upon him, except by the lawful judgment of his peers or by the law of the land." Accordingly, an imprisonment or detention of any kind can always be challenged as unlawful – and that is the essence of the habeas corpus procedure. Anyone who knows about such imprisonment can apply for the writ, and a High Court judge is always available to issue it urgently, ordering the custodian to bring the prisoner before the court and show the legal basis of imprisonment. Unless satisfactory justification is provided, the prisoner must be freed by the court there and then.

All this seems simple and natural enough; but history is full of examples of how great political and economic interests were smashed to pieces by a writ of habeas corpus. It was by using habeas corpus that the Common Law courts fought and won their jurisdictional war with the terrible Court of High Commission and other Courts of Equity ('equity' as opposed to the common law). The Common Law judges would not recognise their jurisdiction to imprison people for breach of their injunctions, and as a rule, would not miss an opportunity to free their prisoners by habeas corpus.

In Somersett's Case (1772) ( (1772) 20 State Tr 1, (1772) Lofft 1), a certain customs officer bought a black slave in America and brought him to England. The slave, Somersett, was kept in a ship bound for Jamaica when his 'imprisonment' was challenged on Habeas Corpus. Although slavery was widespread in many parts of the Empire, the captain of the ship (represented, like the other side, by some of the most eminent lawyers of the age) could provide no proper justification of it in English law. So the Court of King's Bench ordered Somersett's release. Because of the common law rules of precedent, this meant no less than an outright prohibition of slavery anywhere in England and Wales. Upon setting his foot on English soil, any slave would now become free - 93 years before Abraham Lincoln's emancipation of the slaves in the USA.

Another celebrated constitutional case of the same era was that of, Entick v Carrington (1765); which highlighted other aspects of the Rule of Law. The case was essentially that the Government had no legal right to issue a search warrant against the subject (in that particular case, against a political pamphleteer John Entick in order to suppress alleged sedition). Lord Chief Justice Camden gave judgement for Entick, and held this government's practice of issuing such warrants over the past 80 years to have been unlawful:

*"If it is law, it will be found in our books. If it is not to be found there, it is not law.*

So, the rule of law as understood on the basis of Entick v Carrington includes the following practical elements:

•      The law is entirely blind to the government policy and to any reasons of state – indeed to any political considerations.

•      Long-standing practices of the government may still be illegal, even if tolerated by the subjects and the courts over many decades. Time does not make them legal.

•      The law, on the other hand, recognises constitutional rights of the subjects, such as the right to property or personal liberty; and gives a high priority to the protection of those rights.

•      Every official is personally responsible for the lawfulness of his actions. It is no defence for him that such were his orders or that he was acting in an official capacity.

The last of those principles has been particularly important in shaping our constitution, and stands in stark contrast to continental systems of law. Most other legal systems, as well as the international law, recognise the doctrine of 'state immunity'. As a rule, an official or a former official cannot be prosecuted or sued in an ordinary way for things he did as an agent of the state.

The English law knows no such immunity. On the contrary, power and responsibility are inseparable; and once you are vested with any amount of power, the corresponding amount of responsibility goes with it. Like anybody else, any official may be sued for trespass, theft ('conversion' in Civil Law), false imprisonment, malicious prosecution, etc. He may be imprisoned for contempt of court; until recently, he could be executed for high treason – not an extraordinary end of many political careers in English history. Contrast that with the fact that officers of Europol (the EU's police force) today enjoy immunity for anything they do or say in the course of the their duties – including while on English soil.

In English law, it has always been considered right and proper that a position of power must be an uncomfortable position, and this approach is reflected in many aspects of our Constitution. For example, judges are selected from the best lawyers; but they are paid far less than lawyers of their level would earn in private practice. The whole system is designed to discourage self-interested people from assuming a position of power. The same approach was taken to its extreme with the highest political offices: those who dare to draw the symbolic sword of the State and use coercion against their countrymen must, by doing so, literally risk their heads.

This ruthless model of ministerial responsibility survived, in essence, till very recently, when the New Labour and the Cameron Tory governments sunk into the very opposite of it. Any fault was now blamed on the advice of faceless civil servants (who, by convention, could not even answer); if the fault was particularly monstrous, a named civil servant was made a scapegoat. This was a murder of the noble constitutional tradition whereby every Minister was personally responsible for everything happening in his department, with or without his knowledge or consent. An oversight by a civil servant mandated the resignation of a Minister, to give way to someone who would be able to better manage his servants. A resignation, indeed, was not even a punishment, but rather an escape. For culpable misconduct or corruption by the Minister himself, the liability was criminal; and the penalty for high treason was death.

There is nothing sentimentalist about justice. Our ruthless constitutional doctrine of ministerial responsibility would be condemned, without hesitation, by any modern Employment Tribunal, not to mention the European Court of Human Rights. Yet without it, we would have never developed democracy. And if any further defence of it is needed, we should only recall the names of its last victims: statesmen whom a British judge ruthlessly sent to the gallows merely for the way in which they exercised their ministerial powers. Their names were Hermann Goering, Joachim von Ribbentrop, Alfred Rosenberg, and many others.

Indeed, the Nuremberg Trial was the latest great landmark in the history of the rule of law. It did involve a major legal controversy.

The Nazi leaders operated within the continental legal tradition, which views law as no more than a creature of the state, a 'command of the prince'. They were, perhaps, the most consistent followers Justinian ever had: whatever pleased the Fuhrer had the force of law. Sure enough, being Germans, they had put their legislation in perfect order, had followed the correct procedure to repeal or suspend the inconvenient laws, and had passed sufficient Enabling Acts to enable almost anything. Each of them acted within the powers conferred on him by legislation, and in strict accordance with its relevant provisions and paragraphs. Furthermore, each acted in official capacity and under the orders of superiors; if there ever was a case for state immunity, it was this. From the point of view of a continental lawyer, they were innocent.

Of course, one could always rely on our Soviet allies to hang them anyway. But to pass a lawful judgement upon them, one needed common law judges from Britain and America - judges who knew that there was a Law above and beyond legislation, and that no 'state immunity' or 'order of the prince' could shield one from responsibility for his own actions.

The Nuremberg judgement was thus a victory of the Common Law over the continental legal positivism. There have been those who criticised it as a mere 'lynching party' of victors against the conquered, or excused it as an exceptional procedure adapted in exceptional circumstances to punish exceptional evils. But in truth, it was a triumph of justice which needs no such excuses. The common law nations applied to Germany the same law they had always applied to themselves; and passed the same sentence over German ministers which had so often been passed over English ministers. Every public official in England, from the Prime Minister to the lowest clerk in the borough council, bears legal responsibility for his actions no lesser than that of defendants at Nuremberg trials. The rest is simply a question of punishment fitting the crime.

There is only one exception to that principle, and that is an exception which proves the rule. The English version of 'state immunity' is the Royal Immunity. It begins and ends with the monarch. 'The King can do no wrong' says the maxim of law, which sounds rather despotic and may, indeed, be rooted in the despotism of some forgotten ancient times. It is all the more remarkable how the common law, on consistent application of its first principles, has turned this maxim inside out. For many centuries now, 'the King can do no wrong' means simply that no official can justify his illegal actions by the orders of the state (the King). He cannot escape responsibility by saying he was under King's orders, because the King can do no wrong, so his illegal orders are always void.

Taking the same principle to its logical conclusion, the development of the Constitution reached the point when the monarch has hardly any real power and only acts on advice of others. Those who advise her are fully responsible, with their heads if necessary. But the Queen can do no wrong, she cannot be held responsible, and under the English Constitution it inevitably follows that she has no real power – except the power as the embodiment and Guardian of the Constitution. It is her duty to uphold the Constitution, and therefore to reject unconstitutional advice from her Ministers when she knows it to be so.

## MISUNDERSTANDING OF SOVEREIGNTY

The first and foremost principle of our Constitution is the Rule of Law. It is no exaggeration to say that nearly every government in our history was, at times, annoyed with this. Yet they could not abolish the Constitution. What they could do, and did, was to employ clever lawyers to help them get round it. They found a loophole. We will consider the particulars of their legal trick in a moment; but the result of it was a theory which turned the whole Constitution upside down. They could not deny the Rule of Law; what they could do, and did, was to play with definitions of law.

What is law? To our ancestors, the anonymous and countless co-authors of our Constitution, the answer was certain, albeit a little complex. The Rule of law meant the rule of Common Law – the law of this country since time immemorial, the law so ancient that some considered it to be eternal, whose historic origins could not be ascertained, but whose exact substance was known from the chain of judicial precedents running back to the Conquest and beyond. This idea of law is slightly complex, but it is true, and it has worked. Indeed, it has worked miracles. From the basic laws of nature, from moral commandments of Christianity, from the obscure customs of a forgotten age, it has created the modern democracy.

The new theory is simpler than that, but not necessarily better. We are told that our legitimate and ultimate law-givers are a certain six hundred and forty five people, crowding in the Palace of Westminster like monkeys in the ruins of an ancient temple; and whatever they vote for is law. It matters not, we are told, that the vast majority of them are just lobby-fodder controlled and corralled by the executive government. Nor does it matter, we are told, that most of the legislation they produce are simply rubber-stamped Directives they receive from the European Union and are obliged to transpose into Acts of Parliament. Once they have exercised their rubber-stamp it becomes the law of the land.

This sounds a little counter-intuitive; but if you employ a team of best QCs to argue this for you, they will put it in elegant and persuasive terms. Better still, it may become fashionable among legal academics, who would then hammer it into the heads of law-students. In a couple of generations, as the students grow to become eminent barristers and judges, it would become a dogma of constitutional law.

Something very much like this has really happened in England in the late 19th century and the early 20th. The Liberal Party was moving rapidly to the Left, and increasingly embraced the then fashionable philosophies of utilitarianism and socialism. The common law constitution, with its emphasis on the rule of law and limited government, seemed to stand in the way of large-scale progressive reforms.

Their ideological icon, Bentham, believed in "the greatest happiness for the greatest number" as the ultimate "measure of right and wrong", and dismissed the idea of individual rights as "nonsense upon stilts". Accordingly, he poured scorn at the sophisticated procedures of the common law which protected that 'nonsense' at the expense of utilitarian efficiency. Bentham worked out complex formulae for precise scientific measurement of individual and collective happiness. He spent many years designing an ideal utilitarian prison, Panopticon, of which he hoped to be appointed the governor. As his plans were never accepted, he developed a theory of "sinister interest" of the King and the aristocracy whose invisible hands blocked all public-spirited projects such as his. He wrote a book to instruct statesmen how to legislate with the objective of 'greatest happiness for the greatest number' always in mind, and disregarding any abstract morality. His ambition in life was to write an ideal utilitarian legal code for all times and all nations, but that work (fortunately perhaps) was never completed.

Needless to say, the natural conservatism of the Common Law caused infinite irritation of Bentham and his followers. His friend and disciple, Professor Austin, then developed a universal theory on the nature of all laws of all nations at all times, which became known as legal positivism. Austin defined the law as a command of the sovereign power, backed by threats of force; and solemnly proved that the law had nothing to do with morality. Many foreign and historical examples did fit well into it, but the English common law was obviously a bit of an exception. It was only half a century later that another brilliant academic in Oxford could squeeze the English Constitution into Austin's theory. He was Professor A. V. Dicey, and he is still regarded as a great authority on English constitutional law.

According to Dicey, Supremacy (or Sovereignty) of the Queen in Parliament means legal omnipotence. Parliament is "the place where that absolute despotic power, which must in all governments reside somewhere, is entrusted by the constitution of these kingdoms". Its legislative power is unlimited, any Act of Parliament is law, and it follows that the Parliament can legally do anything whatsoever. It can change or abolish the Constitution and create a new one. It can abolish itself. It can abolish its sovereignty and pass it on to somebody else.

As an example of this, Dicey cites the Act of the Union, whereby (as he interprets it) the Parliament of England abolished itself, abolished its sovereignty, and passed it on to a new body: the Parliament of Great Britain.

Further, the power of the Parliament may not be limited by the common law or any Acts of earlier Parliaments. A constitutional maxim is that 'no Parliament can bind its successors', and where (as, for example, in the Act of the Union) the earlier Parliament apparently intended to do that, those 'entrenchment' provisions have no legal effect.

The logical inconsistency of this is rather obvious. If the Parliament could do anything up to abolishing its sovereignty, it could also bind its successors, and even prevent their very existence. If it cannot bind its successors, this means it cannot abolish its sovereignty. This is one obvious limit of its power; and if the Constitution sets one such limit, it is equally obvious that the Constitution can, in principle, set other limits. Omnipotence is a paradoxical concept, and the medieval theologians had enough trouble even with the omnipotence of God. No wonder that anyone who tries to assert the omnipotence of the State inevitably runs into the same, and greater, logical problems.

It is not difficult to see that Dicey's theory is based on a manifestly false premise, an infamous superstition of his age: the axiom that some 'absolute despotic power' must 'in all governments reside somewhere'. Of course, the whole point of the English Constitution is that it has never allowed for any 'absolute despotic power' to reside anywhere.

That brings us back to the eternal dilemma of the Book of Kings and of the Nuremberg Trials. The Queen in Parliament does make laws. But then, it is the Law that makes the Queen in Parliament. This said, one or the other, hen or the egg, has to come first. This circle has to be squared, or it will be a vicious circle. The answer cannot really be historic, it will probably be fictional, and yet, there must be a clear answer. If you like, it is either a Divine Right of Kings or a divine origin of the Law. Justinian, Austin and Dicey have given one of the two logically possible answers; but there is obviously the other possibility. And anybody who has read a dozen of English law reports taken at random will see that the choice of our ancestors was different from Professor Dicey's. The Constitution of England places its foundations upon the Rule of Law and not any arbitrary despotic power.

If a state authority could change the law as it pleases, the Rule of Law would be of little substance. It would become merely a question of re-writing the law before breaking it. It would be a question of having enough lawyers to cope. It would be, in brief, merely a question of applying high standards of German efficiency to the work of the legislature. No wonder that the Nazis and Marxists adapted the theory of legal positivism unreservedly. The rest is history, which Dicey perhaps could not foresee, but we ought to remember. Such theories as legal positivism are not innocent witticisms of eccentric professors. They ultimately lead to evil.

A Martian knowing nothing about human society, or a professor looking at it from the height of his ivory tower, may well conclude that a large city like London is dominated by the struggle between several armed gangs, each enforcing their will as 'law', the Metropolitan Police being merely the most successful of them (and even that is open to question). By academic standards, the theory is perfectly plausible; but any Londoner living in a real word would immediately know it is nonsense. He would not need any theoretical argument to see the difference between the policeman and the gangster. Or if he could not actually see it, he would at least know that something has gone quite wrong with the police, and that something has to be done about it.

Anyone who would analyse the English Constitution from the point of view of power, its limits, or the lack of them, falls into the same fallacy. To see how flawed this approach is, one only needs to apply it to English institutions other than Parliament. You will see at once that the Constitution is full of different authorities possessing unlimited or almost unlimited formal powers, and that those vast powers overlap most hopelessly. Yet for some mysterious reason, they are never used.

It is, technically, true that the Parliament has the power to make or unmake any law.

But it is also true that Her Majesty the Queen technically has the legal powers to veto all new legislation henceforward, to dissolve the government tomorrow, to abolish the Cabinet and the office of the Prime Minister, to appoint a military junta for a government, to denounce all the international treaties ever signed, and to declare a war to reconquer the Holy Land. As the head of the Church, she can also make it a crusade. Quite seriously, she has the 'legal' power to do all these things overnight; but if she is really advised to do that, that advice might be, with some reason, criticised as unconstitutional.

It is also true that the Courts of Law have the exclusive power to decide what is and what is not the law of the land. That inevitably includes the powers to hold Acts of Parliament void, to burn heretics, or to condemn all bankers to death (usury being a crime under the Law of God, they might say). I deliberately refrain from making up more unreasonable examples. Further, they have a power to make any injunction they think to be 'just and convenient', i. e. to order anybody whomsoever to do or not to do anything whatsoever, and to commit people to prison for disobedience to such orders (contempt of court). That power is as 'unlimited' as the legislative power of Parliament. They have the power to do all these things, and more; but if they really made full use of that power, there would be some scope for an argument that the power had been abused.

Last not least, we, the Queen's subjects, also have constitutional powers we should be rather slow to use - for example, in principle, the right to a lawful armed rebellion against any government in breach of the Magna Carta. But if we really care about the Constitution, we should try and find more peaceful means to preserve it. As a matter of law, the right to a lawful rebellion is there. And yet, it is there not for use, but for deterrent.

These elementary examples make it quite obvious that a Dicey-style measurement of legal power does not help us to understand our Constitution at all. If, in practice, our constitutional mechanism has worked like clockwork for many centuries, this was not due to such legally defined borderlines as Dicey sought but failed to discover for the powers of Parliament. Rather, it is based on the legal distinction between 'use' and 'abuse' of power. It is based on what medieval lawyers meant when they said the law was all about 'rights' and 'wrongs' (and it is our own fault that we have now forgotten half of the equation). It is a much more sophisticated mechanism than a mere balance of naked power. Taken out of this context, the legal powers of Parliament or any other institution are nonsense upon stilts.

To be fair, Dicey himself realised and acknowledged that his theory was an oversimplification. In the best academic traditions, he named his book Introduction into the Study of the Law of the Constitution, and opened it by a reservation that this was only an introduction, that oversimplifications were inevitable, and that anyone who wants to have a proper understanding of the Constitution should instead read the four volumes of Commentaries by Mr. Justice Blackstone (who wrote something totally different). Yet, Dicey's book was so short, simple, lightly written, that year after year, the law students – perhaps having spent the whole term in careless abandon would find it invaluable for the last night before the dreaded exam in constitutional law.

Yet, to understand the right and proper place of Parliament in our constitution, we have to look elsewhere. We cannot, obviously, go through the detailed history of how and by whom it was created; but we can reasonably briefly explain why.

## GOVERNMENT BY CONSENT

John Reeves, Esq., a retired judge, an eminent legal historian, the founder of the Association for Preserving Liberty and Property against Republicans and Levellers (based in the Crown and Anchor pub on the Strand, London), and (as subsequently emerged from the indictment) "a malicious, seditious and ill-disposed person greatly disaffected to the government of this realm" – this Mr Reeves, in 1795, published a pamphlet called, Thoughts on the English Government, addressed to the quiet good sense of the People of England in a series of Letters. That pamphlet discussed the same subject as the present work: the Constitution. Among other things,

Mr. Reeves made a point that the King was the ultimate source of all legal power in England, and proceeded to illustrate it with a metaphor:

*"In fine (the End), the government of England is a monarchy: the Monarch is the ancient stock from which have sprung those goodly branches of the Legislature, the Lords and Commons, that at the same time give ornament to the Tree, and afford shelter to those who seek protection under it. But these are still only branches, and derive their origin and their nutriment from their common parent; they may be lopped off, and the Tree is a Tree still; shorn indeed of its honours, but not, like them, cast into the fire. The kingly government may go on, in all its functions, without Lords or Commons: it has heretofore done so for years together, and in our times it does so during every recess of parliament; but without the king his parliament is no more. The king, therefore, alone it is who necessarily subsists without change or diminution, and from him alone we unceasingly derive the protection of law and government."*

The House of Commons were quite unhappy with Mr. Reeves's apparent dissension from the 'Whig version of history', and especially with the suggested theoretical possibility of their being "cast into the fire" while George III would only be "shorn of honours". So much so that they passed a resolution compelling the reluctant Attorney General to prosecute Mr. Reeves for seditious libel. That he did, only to have the enthusiast for monarchy acquitted by the jury. (T. B. Howell. A complete collection of State Trials and proceedings for high treason and other crimes and misdemeanors. London, 1819. Vol. XXVI, p.p. 529-596.)

Of course, Mr. Reeves was right. The starting point of our Constitution is that all the state power originally lies with the monarch – 'Our Sovereign Lady the Queen'. At the same time, the Queen can do no wrong; and to be quite sure of that, she is not supposed to do anything of her own motion. She only acts on advice. Those who give that advice are the real decision-makers; consequently the advisors bear all the responsibility. The recurrent battle-cry of all rebellions in our history was rescuing the monarch from evil counsellors.

Even in the stormy 17th century, the century of revolutions and civil wars, the fiercest critics of the Crown would only demand at their fiercest moments: "those who gave this advice to the King must pay with their heads".

We are used to thinking of the 1640s Civil War as that between the King and the Parliament; but the parties viewed it differently. The Cavaliers fought for the King in Parliament against what in their view were a bunch of renegade and rebellious MPs, the only lawful Parliament consisting of the loyalist Lords and MPs assembled by the King in Oxford. The Roundheads fought for the legal fiction of a King in Parliament against the 'King in royalist camp' - the person of the King being imprisoned by evil counsellors, but his legal self as the living symbol of the Constitution being obviously on the right side. The most anti-monarchist period of our history was all about the Roundheads' relentless efforts to find a way not to execute the King, and instead blame those advising him. This was not because they were in any degree sentimental about Charles I, but because they respected the Constitution. Once they lost patience and killed the King, they immediately saw the entire constitutional edifice collapsing - and were buried under its ruins.

So, much of our Constitution consists of the rules on advising the monarch, who is allowed to advise in what circumstances, and how that advice be given and taken. Thus, every Act of Parliament begins with the words: "Be It Enacted by the Queen's Most Excellent Majesty, by and with the advice and consent of the Lords Spiritual and Temporal, and the Commons, in the Present Parliament Assembled". A government decision, constitutionally, is the advice given to Her Majesty by the Cabinet, which is an informal committee in her Privy Council. Our top judges, hearing cases as the Judicial Committee of the Privy Council, conclude their judgements by "humbly advising Her Majesty to dismiss this appeal".

So, inevitably, the Queen has many faces in the Constitution, depending on who gives advice. The authority of the Crown is one thing. The authority of the Queen in Council is another. The authority of the Queen in Parliament is altogether different.

It was accepted for many centuries that the authority of the Queen in Parliament is supreme to all others, since the advice of the both Houses carries more weight than any other advice Her Majesty may ever receive. The Queen out of Parliament ranks lower than the Queen in Parliament, and in this sense, only the Queen in Parliament is truly sovereign. This is why constitutional lawyers talk of 'parliamentary sovereignty' or 'sovereignty of Parliament' (meaning that Parliament consisting of the two Houses and the monarch). But in the strict sense, it is the Sovereignty of the Queen in Parliament; or simply the Sovereignty of the Queen, re-enforced by the parliamentary advice and consent.

We shall discuss consent in a moment, but pausing here, it is clear that if the Queen is 'under the law', she has to be 'under the law' in all her roles, whoever gives the advice, be it in or out of Parliament. It would be somewhat absurd to squeeze the law into the constitutional hierarchy somewhere in between, just above the Queen and just below the Queen in Parliament.

In many other democracies, 'we, the people' are declared to be an absolute sovereign and the source of all power. The legal foundations of English democracy are quite different – in a sense, the very opposite of that. The Sovereign and the Subject are different legal personalities; but the constitutional relationship between them is governed by the Law, and accordingly they have mutual rights and duties.

In Calvin's Case (1608), Sir Edward Coke, then Lord Chief Justice of Common Pleas, and 'all of the judges of England' (meaning, in modern terms, all the 12 Law Lords), held ((1608) 7 Coke Reports 2a; quoting from: The Selected Writings and Speeches of Sir Edward Coke, ed. Steve Sheppard (Indianapolis: Liberty Fund, 2003). Vol. 1.; the text in square brackets is English translation of Latin quotations.):

*1. That ligeance, or obedience of the subject to the Sovereign, is due by the Law of nature: 2. That this Law of nature is part of the Laws of England: 3. That the Law of nature was before any judicial or municipal Law in the world: 4. That the Law of nature is immutable and cannot be changed...*

*So as between the Sovereign and subject there is [a dual and
reciprocal tie, because just as the subject is bound in obedience
to the king, so the king is bound to the protection of the subject;
and therefore allegiance is properly so called from ligando (tying)
because it contains within itself a two-way tie]. And therefore it
is holden in 20 H. 7, 8. that there is a liege or ligeance between
the King and the subject. And Fortescue, (Chap. 13): [the King
is made in order to safeguard the law, the bodies and the goods
of the subjects.] And in the Acts of Parliament... subjects are
called liege people, and... the King is called the liege Lord of his
Subjects...*

Ligeance is the mutual bond and obligation between the King and
his subjects, whereby subjects are called his liege subjects, because
they are bound to obey and serve him, and he is called their liege
Lord, because he should maintain and defend them. Whereby it
appeareth, that in this point the Law of England, and of Scotland is
all one. Therefore it is truly said that [protection attracts subjection,
and subjection protection.]

Some, in their ignorance, might consider this to be a medieval
doctrine based on outdated feudal rights and of no relevance today;
but such a view would smash to pieces the entire modern international
law as well as the constitutional law of many nations.

Take, for instance, the US Declaration of Independence, which
directly refers to the Calvin's Case doctrine by accusing the King:
'He has abdicated government here by declaring us out of his
protection and waging war against us.' Unless we recognise the
validity of Calvin's Case doctrine, we have to maintain that the
Declaration of Independence is void, the United States have no legal
existence, and still remains our colony – a rebellious colony though
it may be. I doubt that anybody in their right mind would maintain
that nowadays.

But forget the US independence; in 2011 the United Kingdom and
many other nations declared a war on Libya on the basis of that very
legal doctrine – indeed, a rather far-fetched interpretation of it, termed
by the UN 'Responsibility to protect'. Their legal case against

Comrade Gaddafi was identical to the Declaration of Independence case against George III: that he had waged a war on his own people, abandoned the state's responsibility to protect them, and thus abdicated the sovereign government of Libya. It is a dispute outside our present purposes whether the Calvin's Case doctrine was correctly interpreted here, and whether it goes far enough to warrant a war in support of a 'lawful rebellion' – if a lawful rebellion it was. The point is that the doctrine itself is still universally recognized today. It is as valid as it was in 1608.

That legal doctrine is as fundamental to our Constitution as it is to the American one. It has many remarkable and far-reaching implications, including, indeed, the right to a lawful rebellion in certain extreme circumstances – which is also re-asserted in many celebrated constitutional documents from Magna Carta to the US Declaration of Independence. But perhaps the greatest debt we owe to that doctrine is that it created our Democracy while also preserving the Monarchy.

While the Subject owed the general duty of obedience to his Sovereign, he also had such rights and liberties which the Sovereign has no power to limit or violate. Hence, there are certain things that can only be done by consent between the Sovereign and the Subject. One notable example is taxation.

The reason is that taxation violates property rights of the Subject. It may sound surprising in our age, after a century dominated by socialist dogma, but property rights rank very high in the Common Law, and our entire legal history reflects an extremely careful approach to protecting them. This is why Magna Carta 1215 provides in c. 12: 'No scutage nor aid shall be imposed on our kingdom, unless by common counsel of our kingdom'.

Then, in c. 14, it is explained what is meant by the common counsel of the kingdom and how the monarch can obtain it. He should summon 'the archbishops, bishops, abbots, earls, and greater barons' and 'all others who hold of us in chief, for a fixed date, namely, after the expiry of at least forty days, and at a fixed place… And when the summons has thus been made, the business shall proceed on the day appointed, according to the counsel of such as are present, although not all who were summoned have come.'

It is fairly well-known that the Parliament as we know it is a direct descendant of that 'general council of the realm'. It is often said that Magna Carta did not provide for such a wide democracy as we are supposed to enjoy now: all it did was enfranchise barons, not the whole populace. However, it is obvious from the very text of Magna Carta that it requires more, not less, than the modern Parliaments deliver. "All others who hold of us in chief" referred to all lieges of the King – in modern terms, all citizens (or at least all households) – who in principle have a right to participate in the Parliament directly, not merely to elect representatives. In strict terms, what Magna Carta requires for obtaining the consent of the people is not a parliament, but we can argue, a referendum.

Of course, referendums were not practicable in the Middle Ages, and the number of King's lieges was too great for such a council even in King John's time. Some kind of reasonable substitute had to be developed. It was found in certain legal fictions imported from the law of the Church - the legal fictions we know under such names as 'representation' or 'constituency'. The constituents were deemed to have given their consent through elected representatives, as they could not all give it in person. Such is the origin of the House of Commons.

The development of English democracy over the next eight centuries was driven by acute and troubling understanding that the House of Commons was only a substitute; tormented by the fear that it is not representative enough. The electoral system was changed many times to widen the franchise, and never to narrow it. People are widely dissatisfied with the present first-past-the-post system as well, and for exactly the same reason: the Parliament so elected is an inadequate instrument for obtaining such a general consent of the realm as required by the Constitution.

Even more to the point are all the constitutional conventions concerning electoral manifestos, whereby a manifesto promise is considered as binding on the government. Consequently, it is constitutionally appropriate to 'whip' MPs to vote to fulfil a manifesto pledge people have voted for, and utterly unconstitutional to 'whip' them to vote to breach it. House of Lords never blocks or delays legislation fulfilling a manifesto promise.

Finally, a government which has lost a vote, or fears to lose a vote, in the Parliament, can 'go to the country' and initiate a general election on a single issue. The system works exactly like an appeal from a lower court to a higher one, whose decision is final.

All these conventions were designed to cure the obvious deficiency of the Parliament: it is a substitute. The English Constitution requires more than advice and consent of a parliament to raise taxes or change the law. It requires advice and consent of the whole realm. Nothing can be further from the truth than an assertion, advanced by some, that the English Constitution is based on parliamentary government and does not require any referendums. Referendum is one thing it demands in most clear terms, in a constitutional act of paramount authority. If anything, it is the parliament, not the referendum, which is unconstitutional.

Contrary to modern theories, Parliament is not there to govern by divine right; even less so to put the stamp of divine approval to the decrees of usurpers. It is there solely to give effect to the constitutional principle of government by consent. There was a time when it was the only practical form for the fullest possible realisation of that principle. Whether it remains so today is a big question to say the least.

## THE HIGH COURT OF PARLIAMENT

When a modern parliamentarian wants to annoy his colleagues, he only needs to mention the well-established legal fact that the Parliament is a Court. They do it quite often, always with a preliminary reservation: "I know everybody nowadays balks if you mention the High Court of Parliament, and yet, I have decided to annoy you."

I am not sure why it is supposed to annoy anyone; certainly not because it is a historic phrase of no modern relevance, which it is not.

To a layman's mind, a court is a place swarming with clever lawyers tirelessly getting round the law. Parliament passes this test with flying colours. But it is also a court in a much more formal sense. Only four years ago, until the anti-constitutional reform of New Labour took effect, the Parliament was a Court of Law hearing cases just like any other. It was a perfectly modern court wherein perfectly modern lawyers brought perfectly modern appeals, having previously lost in the High Court or the Court of Appeal. By convention, the appeals were heard by a panel of Law Lords, sitting in one of the committee rooms as the Judicial Committee of the House of Lords. Yet there was no doubt that they performed the judicial duties of the Queen in Parliament on her behalf. All lawyers refer to their judgements simply as 'House of Lords decisions', without mentioning any committees.

Separation of powers is, of course, present in the English Constitution, but not at such an exaggerated scale as its foreign admirers assumed when they copied it in America and France. Executive and the Legislature are separated by the distinction between Queen in Parliament and Queen in Council. Yet, while in America it is almost mandatory that these two branches be controlled by different parties, here, it is mandatory that they are controlled by the same party. Judiciary and Legislature were separated by putting the Law Lords in a distinct committee room, but not by creating a separate Supreme Court as was done by the Americans, the French, and the New Labour. Executive and Judiciary were separated by prohibiting the King to adjudicate cases without judges; yet the King was allowed to preside over judges both in House of Lords and in the Court of King's Bench. In brief, separation of power is a valuable principle of the English Constitution, but it often has to give way to another and more fundamental one.

There is no principle more fundamental than the Rule of Law. As natural consequence of it, our entire civil administration was originally administration of justice, a government by the Courts of Law. In a medieval English county, there was no state authority to be found except justices of the peace. They made the less important decisions at 'petty sessions', which we know today as Magistrates

Courts; and more important decisions at 'quarter sessions' which we know as Crown Courts. Above them, there were the royal courts performing the judicial duties of the King in Council, such as the Courts of King's Bench, Chancery, Admiralty, etc. – all now amalgamated into the High Court of Justice. And at the top, there was the High Court of Parliament. This is obviously not intended as a complete description of the medieval hierarchy of courts

It is all quite logical and obvious that if you want to live under the rule of law, you need a system of courts; that this system needs to be hierarchical so that mistakes of lower courts could be corrected on appeal to higher ones; and that the ladder of appeals has to end somewhere. If there is an appeal from a Magistrates Court to the High Court, and then from a High Court to the House of Lords, there must be one court at the top whose decision is final and cannot be challenged elsewhere.

In a more medieval language, when wronged by your local justices of the peace, you appeal to the Queen; when wronged by the Queen, you appeal to the Queen in Parliament. But there was no authority higher than the Queen's Most Excellent Majesty acting by and with the advice and consent of the Lords Spiritual and Temporal, and the Commons, in the present Parliament assembled. Consequently, the decision of Parliament was final and there was no further appeal. This is the true origin and meaning of parliamentary supremacy.

If you look at the old parliamentary rolls and statute books, you will discover that for most of our history, there was hardly any distinction between the Acts of Parliament and its judicial decisions. Most Acts of Parliament were so-called 'private acts', addressing someone's private grievances, e. g. to legitimise such and such a bastard, to naturalise such and such alien, to dispossess such and such widow, or to hang, draw, and quarter such and such Minister of the Crown. The monarch would then gracefully direct that the minister should only be hanged, but spared from drawing and quartering. But the 'public acts' of old Parliaments, i. e. those on matters of importance to the whole country or a large part of it, also look like judicial decisions, explaining why the present state of affairs was inconsistent with the common law and ordering how it should be remedied. Of course, these statutes of Parliament became part of the law – in the same way as any judicial precedent is part of the common law.

The original distinction was simply this. Some of the decisions, such as judgements on purely legal appeals, could be made by the King and the Lords without the 'consent of the kingdom'. Others required a greater authority, for they diminished liberty or property of the subjects, e.g. involved taxation, and therefore required consent of the Commons. All Acts of Attainder, i. e. death sentences by the High Court of Parliament, required the consent of the Commons. They were the jury in that Court; and like lower courts, the Parliament could make the more important judgements only after a trial by jury, and the less important ones (e.g. on purely legal points) without a jury. Such is the origin of the Acts of Parliament on one hand and judgements of the House of Lords on the other, both being decisions of the same court.

As explained above, in our Constitution the law is not 'made', but 'found' in judicial precedents following earlier judicial precedents, following still earlier ones, etc. It is natural that a precedent judgement of a higher Court should be binding on the lower ones. Hence is the rule, whose origin and meaning is now widely misunderstood, that no court will question the validity of an Act of Parliament, and only the Parliament itself can overrule it. All the courts can do with an Act of Parliament or a binding precedent is to interpret it narrowly, if justice so requires.

But it has always been a much more difficult question whether a court should be bound by its own earlier decisions. Different courts in different ages developed different rules on that. The problem is that of balance: liberty to disregard the precedent would leave little of the law, but too rigid adherence to the precedent could cause injustice. After all, no system is perfect, and it did happen that the ancient judges erred in stating the law to be applied several centuries later to circumstances they could not imagine. Surprisingly though, this happened very rarely. Rules of precedent changed with time; but the overall spirit has always been that the courts must stick to the precedent if at all possible, re-interpret it if necessary, and only depart from it in most exceptional cases where there is a very good reason to do so.

Obviously, the dilemma was most acute at the top of the pyramid. A lower court can follow the precedent even if it leads to injustice, in reliance on the right of appeal to a higher court which has the proper authority to overrule the precedent. Yet the Parliament could not do that – it had to make the final decision, and it had to be just. Hence is the rule that 'no Parliament can bind its successors' and its power 'to make or unmake any law'. But it is not supposed to be an arbitrary power, and never was.

One of the basic principles of Statute Law is the distinction between declaratory and remedial statutes. To quote Mr. Justice Blackstone:

*Statutes… are either declaratory of the common law, or remedial of some defects therein. Declaratory, where the old custom of the kingdom is almost fallen into disuse, or become disputable; in which case the parliament has thought proper, in perpetuum rei testimonium [In perpetual testimony of a matter; i. e. for the purpose of declaring and settling a thing forever (Black's Law Dictionary, 2nd ed.)] , and for avoiding all doubts and difficulties, to declare what the common law is and ever hath been. Thus the statute of treasons, 25 Edw. III. cap. 2, doth not make any new species of treasons, but only, for the benefit of the subject, declares and enumerates those several kinds of offence which before were treason at the common law. Remedial statutes are those which are made to supply such defects, and abridge such superfluities, in the common law, as arise either from the general imperfection of all human laws, from change of time and circumstances, from the mistakes and unadvised determinations of unlearned (or even learned) judges, or from any other cause whatsoever. And this being done, either by enlarging the common law, where it was too narrow and circumscribed, or by restraining it where it was too lax and luxuriant, hath occasioned another subordinate division of remedial acts of parliament into enlarging and restraining statutes.* (Commentaries, Vol. 1, p.p. 86-87)

Hence follow elaborate rules of interpretation, different for each class of statutes. Thus, all remedial statutes must be interpreted with reference to the state of the common law before it was enacted, what was the 'mischief... for which the common law did not provide', and what was the intended remedy. (Commentaries, Vol. 1, p.p. 86-87) Moreover, a statute altering the common law was seen as something quite exceptional, so the rules of interpretation were, so to speak, very hostile. The words had to be interpreted as narrowly as possible. (S. E. Thorne. Essays in English Legal History. The Hambledon press, London and Ronceverte, 1985. P.p. 155-170: The Equity of a Statute and Heydon's case. See also Waghan v Anon (1346) Y.B. 20 Edw. III, 2, 198)

Sadly, with the advance of 'legal positivism', those rules have been virtually forgotten, obscured by the monstrous exaggeration of the Parliament's technical power 'to make or unmake any law'. It was presumed that any change of the law could be construed as remedying some kind of mischief. But with all the absurdities we find in the contemporary statutes, this is no longer certain. With such statutes as European Communities Act 1972 (as will be detailed in its proper place further below), it is not only impossible to identify a 'mischief' or a 'remedy', but hardly possible to make any sense of it at all. On proper common law interpretation, it has no meaning and should have no effect.

So, with the benefit of but a glimpse at a larger constitutional picture, the logical fallacies of Dicey and his followers are laid bare. The legal power of any Court of Law is unlimited in the same sense in which the legal power of Parliament is unlimited. It is only restrained by the right of appeal, which in many cases does not exist in lower courts, and never exists in Parliament. After the New Labour reform, with the Law Lords moved across the road from Parliament to the new Supreme Court, there is no appeal from the Supreme Court either. But this does not mean that the judges in the Supreme Court, or any other, are free to govern us by putting all their fancies and lunacies into binding injunctions , another dozen every day, and imprisoning anyone who disobeys them for contempt of court.

In a logical fallacy as old as the world, Dicey (and other modern theorists) get false statements by reversing the true ones. Dicey takes some common law maxim – say "there is no wrong without a remedy" – and interprets it literally as follows: "The maxim… does not mean, as it is sometimes supposed, that there is a legal remedy for every moral or political wrong. If this were its meaning, it would be manifestly untrue… It would be more intelligibly and correctly stated, if it were reversed, so as to stand, 'Where there is no legal remedy, there is no legal wrong'."

By the same logic, he reverses the commonplace that the courts should enforce the law, and concludes: whatever is enforced by the courts is law, and whatever is not enforced by the courts is not law. Now, a lower court obviously cannot enforce anything on a higher court, and none can enforce anything on the High Court of Parliament. Hence, Parliament is above the law, and anything that happens in Parliament is legal by definition.

I do not expect my readers to include many academics, so it is hardly necessary to explain that the law does not exist for the benefit of the courts. It is, to put it crudely, the other way round. This is true about any court, including the High Court of Parliament. And taking the favourite hypothesis of Diceyan theorists, if an Act of Parliament decrees that all blue-eyed babies be murdered, it will not (as they proudly assert) be law. It will be a criminal conspiracy to murder, and all the legal professors in the world cannot make it anything else.

The anonymous authors of the Common Law were no idiots, and when they created such maxims as 'the King never dies', 'the King can do no wrong', or 'there is no wrong without a remedy', they did not mean them as statements of fact. What they meant was a bold but sensible idea that the lawless reality should be brought in line with the law, not vice versa. That is why, having noted that highwaymen have become too numerous, they would apply their vigour to catching and hanging highwaymen, not to reforming the outdated law against robbery or abolishing the death penalty. If the King died, they crowned a new one, and did not abolish monarchy. If there was a wrong, they would find or create a remedy, and not insist that the wrong was somebody's human right. If the King tried to do any wrong, they would not let him do it. And if the government was lawless, they would change the government, not the law. This is what the rule of law means, this is where democracy began, and 'legal positivism' is where they both end.

Our ancestors may have been ignorant of many things, but they were not ignorant of that refreshingly modern idea that the sovereign governs by divine right and whatever pleases him is law. Even without the benefit of learned opinion from modern academics, the medieval judges had somehow heard about that theory – and were not impressed.

## SOVEREIGNTY IN THE ENGLISH CONSTITUTION

At the time our unique system took shape in England, Europe was, in many regards, much more united then it is today. European Union remains essentially a utopian chimera, which only creates ever deeper divisions between the nations of Europe; but Christendom was once a reality. The Church, still united under the undisputed authority of Rome, was seen in those times as a society people lived in rather than a place they went to. Its significance to people's daily lives was much greater than that of any state authority. They still had a common language (Latin) known to all educated people, even if it was not their mother tongue.

The cosmopolitan web of feudal allegiances ran across Europe from Ireland to Poland: it was not extraordinary for the King of England to claim inheritance of the French crown, or for a Duke of Normandy to claim inheritance of the English one, and some of them were liege vassals to one another. And as far as the constitutional law was concerned, continental Europe followed Justinian's principle. At least in theory, the royal power remained absolute, and the law was only there by the command of the prince.

Such was the world in which the unique Common Law Constitution of England was born. It was, at first, a kind of local heresy. To survive, it had to be fenced against the overwhelming influence of Roman constitutional orthodoxy. It had to assert the supremacy of the Crown

*King Henry VIII re-established after some five centuries the principal that the King of England was the ultimate ruler of his realm when he broke with the Catholic Church in Rome and forbade anyone to appeal to a court of law outside those of England. He thus restored to the English crown the "imperium" or right to rule that it had enjoyed before 1066.*

as the embodiment of our peculiar constitution, and to denounce "all foreign jurisdictions, powers, superiorities, and authorities". Hence grew the principle of Sovereignty. In the medieval world where people would talk of Christians and Heathens but almost never of Englishmen, Germans or Italians, the idea of a sovereign nation-state was by no means an obvious idea. Like all common law principles, sovereignty was developed by resolving practical controversies in a fair and logical way protecting the integrity of the law.

We all enjoy those macabre stories about Henry VIII getting tired of an old wife, sending her to the scaffold, and starting all over again with a new one; and how annoyed he was with the Pope refusing him a divorce, so that he eventually sacked the Pope and appointed himself the head of the Church instead. There is some truth in the tales of the tyrant King - and that is why it has grown so exaggerated. But while the facts are for the jury of popular opinion, there is a more serious legal side to it. The argument between the Kings and the Popes went on for over five centuries, both before and after Henry VIII. That argument was not about marriages and divorces, and originally not even about religion – it was about jurisdiction.

In medieval England, all matters whatsoever were divided into 'spiritual' and 'temporal' ones (like members of the House of Lords). Thus there were the spiritual courts of the Church, working under its own law, its own procedures (all very different from the common law), and with appeals to Rome. The frontiers of jurisdiction were blurred. For example, all clergy was exempt from the jurisdiction of temporal common law courts. If a 'clergyman' killed someone, that would be a matter for church courts. 'Clergyman' was defined as anybody who could read or write. To prove he was a clergyman, the defendant in court had only to read the 51st Psalm: Miserere mei, Deus, etc. Needless to say, there may have been one or two criminals who successfully managed to recite the Psalm and escaped the gallows without really being literate, let alone having anything to do with the church.

So this was a country with two different systems of law and of courts, and these were not the most law-abiding people who had most advantage of it. There were gaps which had to be closed, and unsurprisingly, there were always two views on how to do that.

It may appear ironic that King John I, one of the worst and most lawless kings England ever had, should have played so great a part in the development of our constitutional law. Yet, it is natural for the precedent-based Common Law to remember and immortalise the names of its offenders rather than defenders. Likewise, the leading precedent cases asserting the principles of criminal justice bear the names of murderers and thieves. The Common Law requires a breach to re-assert itself; as a consequence, it rewards offenders with immortality.

Magna Carta was a concession wrung from King John in defence of the Common Law Constitution; but about the same time, another great concession was wrung from him in defiance of it. Following his long and bitter conflict with the Pope, John had to yield. On 15th May 1213 in Dover Castle, he surrendered his crown to a papal legate, and received it back as a fief of the Holy See. He was now the Pope's liege, bound to pay annual tribute, and no longer a Sovereign Lord of England; or so it seemed.

*It was under King Edward III that the constitutional principle was established that the monarch holds the kingdom in trust for his successors and so cannot give away his own sovereignty.*

But it is not within the constitutional power of a Sovereign to abolish his Sovereignty. As a matter of law, the kingdom was not his to give away. A century and a half later, in 1366, King Edward III's Parliament held that the King only holds the kingdom on trust for his successors and cannot give it away without the people's consent; consequently, the transaction between John I and the Pope was unconstitutional and void. (40 Edw. III; Blackstone Commentaries, Vol. 4, Ch. 8)

That was one in a series of the anti-Papal Statutes of Provisors and Praemunire enacted by successive kings of the House of Plantagenet throughout the 14th century. Their legal dispute with the Pope was long, complicated, and involved some fine points of feudal law which are of little relevance today; but a few of them now hit the mark precisely. It was then that the criminal offence of Praemunire was introduced, which Blackstone defines as "introducing a foreign power into the land, and creating imperium in imperio (a government within a government), by paying that obedience to papal process, which constitutionally belonged to the king alone" (Commentaries, Vol. 4, Ch. 8). Like its older brother, the offence of High Treason,

Praemunire could take many forms, and a few of them are not without modern relevance (although now repealed):

-       It is Praemunire to "cite the King, or any of his subjects, to answer in the court of Rome", or to appeal against the King or his subjects in any foreign jurisdiction.

-       "whoever procures at Rome, or elsewhere, any translations, processes, excommunications, bulles, instruments, or other things which touch the king, against him, his crown, and realm, and all persons aiding and assisting therein" are guilty of Praemunire under the statute 16 Ric. II. c. 5. (Commentaries, Vol. 4, Ch. 8)

The same controversy renewed in an even sharper form under Tudors. Its constitutional side is well illustrated by the words of the statute 25 Hen. VIII. c. 21 addressed to the King (at the time the Parliament, still true to its older judicial tradition, would give the reasons of its decision in the text of the statute):

*"This your grace's realm, recognising no superior under God but only your grace, hath been and is free from subjection to any man's laws, but only to such as have been devised, made, and ordained within this realm, for the wealth of the same; or to such other as, by sufferance of your grace and your progenitors, the people of this your realm have taken at their free liberty, by their own consent, to be used among them; and have bound themselves by long use and custom to the observance of the same; not as to the observance of the laws of any foreign prince, potentate, or prelate; but as to the customed and ancient laws of this realm, originally established as laws of the same, by the said sufferance, consents, and custom; and none otherwise."* (Commentaries, Vol. 4, Ch. 8)

As we revisit the history of those controversies, we must always keep it in mind that all fine and difficult problems arose over the church government, and the borderlines between spiritual and temporal jurisdictions. Eventually, the supremacy of the King was established in spiritual matters as well as temporal. But no similar disputes ever arose about the temporal government, where the supremacy of the King was absolute and undisputed. The Popes were

*Queen Elizabeth I was one of the most popular of English monarchs. She was remarkably tolerant for her age, but was clear that the monarch of England was supreme within England and insisted on absolute loyalty against foreign states, powers and enemies.*

accused of abusing the rights of the church for introducing a foreign government and foreign laws into the temporal affairs. Rome denied this. But neither party doubted for a moment that introducing a foreign government in temporal affairs was illegal.

The Elizabethan Oath of Supremacy is a good illustration of that: *'I, (name), do utterly testify and declare in my conscience, that the queen's highness is the only supreme governor of this realm, and of all other her highness's dominions and countries,* **as well in all spiritual or ecclesiastical things or causes, as temporal, and that no foreign prince, person, prelate, state or potentate, has, or ought to have, any jurisdiction, power, superiority, preeminence, or authority ecclesiastical or spiritual, within this realm;** *and therefore I do utterly renounce and forsake all foreign jurisdictions, powers, superiorities, and authorities, and do* *promise that from henceforth I shall bear faith and true allegiance to the queen's highness, her heirs and lawful successors, and to my power shall assist and defend all jurisdictions, pre-eminences, privileges, and authorities granted or belonging to the queen's highness, her heirs and successors, or united and annexed to the imperial crown of this realm. So help me God, and by the contents of this book.' [Emphasis added]*

So, while the controversial Statutes extended the monarch's Supremacy to 'ecclesiastical things or causes', the temporal supremacy is cited as an undisputable point of reference. It had been always enshrined in the Common Law.

The Elizabethan and earlier Acts of Supremacy were repealed in 1969, and it is no longer required of each and every officer of the Crown to swear such an oath – they simply swear allegiance to the Queen and her Heirs and Successors, according to law.

There is, however, one exception. A modified Oath of Supremacy has survived in one place where it is still needed: the Privy Council. Each Privy Counsellor, everyone whose name is today preceded by the ironic letters 'Rt. Hon.', anyone who has ever been a Cabinet Minister or a member of a Shadow Cabinet – from the Rt. Hon. Edward Heath to the Rt. Hon. David Cameron – have sworn this:

*"You do swear by Almighty God to be a true and faithful Servant unto the Queen's Majesty, as one of Her Majesty's Privy Council. You will not know or understand of any manner of thing to be attempted, done, or spoken against Her Majesty's Person, Honour, Crown, or Dignity Royal, but you will let and withstand the same to the uttermost of your Power, and either cause it to be revealed to Her Majesty Herself, or to such of Her Privy Council as shall advertise Her Majesty of the same. You will, in all things to be moved, treated, and debated in Council, faithfully and truly declare your Mind and Opinion, according to your Heart and Conscience; and will keep secret all Matters committed and revealed unto you, or that shall be treated of secretly in Council. And if any of the said Treaties or Counsels shall touch any of the Counsellors, you will not reveal it unto him, but will keep the same*

*until such time as, by the Consent of Her Majesty, or of the Council, Publication shall be made thereof. You will to your uttermost bear Faith and Allegiance unto the Queen's Majesty; and will assist and **defend all Jurisdictions, Pre-eminences, and Authorities, granted to Her Majesty, and annexed to the Crown by Acts of Parliament, or otherwise, against all Foreign Princes, Persons, Prelates, States, or Potentates.** And generally in all things you will do as a faithful and true Servant ought to do to Her Majesty. So help you God."* (HC Hansard Vol 317 Col 182) [Emphasis added]

To break this oath, like any oath of allegiance to the Queen, is high treason.

In this sense, the effect of Privy Counsellors' oath is very different from the parliamentary oath of allegiance which the MPs and Lords take. If the Parliament votes for a treasonous act (e.g. to diminish the authority of the Crown in favour of a foreign prince, person, prelate, state, or potentate), MPs and Lords will be protected by the Bill of Rights and parliamentary privilege from being prosecuted for treason. It will be for the Queen herself, as the Guardian of the Constitution, to prevent enactment of the treasonous statute by withholding royal assent.

But parliamentary privilege is merely an exception that confirms the rule. It is unique to Parliament, and there is nothing analogous to it in the Privy Council and the Cabinet. Members of the Cabinet and Privy Council bear full criminal responsibility for treason they commit in their office, and for the advice they give to the Queen. There is no end of precedents for this, as discussed above. Indeed, the oath of supremacy and the offence of treason exist, first and foremost, as ruthless constitutional checks of ministerial power.

High Treason, in Common Law, means any breach of allegiance to the Sovereign. The place of High Treason at the top of any 'hierarchy' of offences in English criminal law follows from the paramount status of the constitutional principles of allegiance and sovereignty, as explained in Calvin's Case. If allegiance is the highest duty of all subjects, a breach of that duty must be regarded as the ultimate crime.

In practice, however, something that is certain enough as a constitutional principle proved to be too vague for a definition of a capital crime. Too often in early Middle Ages, the definition of treason would be arbitrarily extended to execute political opponents of the government of the day.

Treason Act 1351 was enacted to remedy such abuses. The definition of High Treason was limited to several distinct headings. The Act, as in force today, reads:

*Whereas divers Opinions have been before this Time in what Case Treason shall be said, and in what not; the King, at the Request of the Lords and of the Commons, hath made a Declaration in the Manner as hereafter followeth, that is to say;*

*[a] When a Man doth compass or imagine the Death of our Lord the King, or of our Lady his Queen, or of their eldest Son and Heir;*

*[b] or if a Man do violate the King's Wife or the King's eldest Daughter unmarried, or the Wife of the King's eldest Son and Heir;*

*[c] or if a Man do levy War against our Lord the King in his Realm, or be adherent to the King's Enemies in his Realm, giving to them Aid and Comfort in the Realm, or elsewhere, and thereof be probably attainted of open Deed by the People of their Condition;*

*[d] and if a Man slay the Chancellor, Treasurer, or the King's Justices of the one Bench or the other, Justices in Eyre, or Justices of Assise, and all other Justices assigned to hear and determine, being in their Places, doing their Offices:*

*And it is to be understood, that in the Cases above rehearsed, that ought to be judged Treason which extends to our Lord the King, and his Royal Majesty.*

Several later Treason statutes made a few amendments to this list. Thus, the Treason Act 1702 made it a high treason to

[e] "endeavour to deprive or hinder any Person who shall be the next in Succession to the Crown [under the Bill of Rights and the Act of Settlement] from succeeding after the Decease of Her Majesty

(whom God long preserve) to the Imperial Crown of this Realm and the Dominions and Territories thereunto belonging". And most importantly, Treason Act 1795 made it treasonable to:

[f] engage in actions "tending to the overthrow of the laws, government and happy constitution" of the United Kingdom.

One is hardly surprised that one of the first actions of the Blair government in 1997 was to repeal Treason Act 1795. Nevertheless, the remaining kinds of High Treason (if they were ever prosecuted nowadays) would be sufficient to safeguard the Constitution. In this sense, the most important is the first heading – Treason by compassing or imagining the death of the King or Queen.

Of course, simply 'imagining' something in literal sense of the word can never be a criminal offence in English law. The courts have always interpreted this kind of treason as requiring an overt act. However, in line with more general principles of criminal law, a conspiracy or incitement would be enough to constitute such an overt act.

In the case of R v Sheanes (1798) (27 St. Tr. 255, 387), the Lord Chief Justice, Lord Carleton, held that treason by compassing and imagining the death of the Sovereign included *"forming conspiracies to usurp by force and in defiance of the authority of Parliament, the government of the kingdom, to destroy its constitution and in so doing to destroy the monarchy"*, e. g. *"holding consultations or entering into agreement, or advising, soliciting or persuading others for any such purposes, or assenting to such purposes"*. Because *"the moment the power of the government is usurped, the king is in effect deposed; he is bound by the duty of his situation to resist such attempts, even at the peril of his life, and several acts which I have mentioned whereby his life may be endangered, have been deemed under the sound construction of the statutes, and upon principles of substantial political justice, overt acts of compassing his death"*. See also the Law Commission Working Paper No 72, 2nd programme, item XVIII, Codification of the Criminal law. Treason, Sedition, and allied offences. London, Her Majesty's Stationery Office, 1977.

This is the modern relevance of high treason, which is an offence against the Constitution rather than the monarch personally. Indeed, the monarch is but a living embodiment of the Constitution, and her sovereignty effectively means supremacy of the Constitution, closely tied to the principle of the Rule of Law. In asserting the sovereignty of the Crown, the Common Law simply defends itself.

This is why exactly the same principles were applied to foreign usurpations and domestic ones. The Common Law would vigorously defend its jurisdiction against any Papal courts, but in the same way, and for the same reason, it would defend its jurisdiction against any non-common-law courts of the sovereign King, such as the Start Chamber. Nor would it allow for an existence of any legislature, capable of changing the law, except the High Court of Parliament which crowned the hierarchy of common law courts. This is why the very same judges who ruthlessly limited the powers of the Sovereign at home would vigorously defend his supremacy against all foreign authorities. This is the exact opposite of what they are doing now.

## THE GREAT CHARTERS

Some sources (though not undisputed by historians) assert that in 1070, four years after the Conquest, King William summoned twelve learned noblemen from every English shire to declare, under oath, the laws and customs of the realm as they were in the times of St. Edward the Confessor.

This does sound somewhat incredible in our times, when the government claims an absolute privilege to tell us what the law is. If a modern democracy never asks its citizens any questions about the

SEAL OF WILLIAM I.

*The seal of King William I shows him in the two roles expected of a medieval king: A warrior protecting his people and a judge administering the law of his kingdom.*

law, surely the warlike medieval King would not ask such questions to his conquered subjects.

Yet, in those times he would have a different understanding of what the law is or should be. Whether the story is factually correct or not, it would be natural for King William to do what it suggests. He knew he was a stranger and a conqueror, yet he considered himself a legitimate King of England by the grace of God, certainly not a tyrant or an usurper. As a King, it was his duty to uphold the ancient laws and usages of the realm; as a foreign conqueror, he found that to be a difficult task. Nothing could be more natural for him than to ask the learned locals what those laws and usages were. The idea that he could make his own laws, apart from some minor amendments, would sound like madness to him. On one hand, he had no taste for such a job; on the other, that would be needlessly oppressive and eventually cause him trouble - for no good reason.

Sure enough, that trouble came soon, to haunt King William's successors for a few centuries. In that stormy period of our history, 'Laws of Edward the Confessor' became a prominent point of reference. Historians are fairly certain that King Edward the Confessor hardly ever enacted any new legislation; the phrase refers

*The coronation of Harold II, last Anglo-saxon King of England. His death at the battle of Hastings in 1066 brought in the Norman age and the development of English law firmly based in its Anglo Saxon roots.*

to the law as it was (or was presumed to have been) before the conquest and since times immemorial.

The tradition portrays the age of first Norman kings as a struggle of the people to defend their ancient liberties against the legislative whims of a foreign dynasty. Thus, one of Henry II's opponents, Ralph Niger, describes the causes of their dispute with the King in his Chronicle ; one of the principal grievances was constitutional - 'he abolished old laws and every year issued new ones' (which, of course, sounds very liberal by modern standards).

In the frequent civil wars of those times, Kings and Pretenders would often issue Charters, pledging to uphold the ancient law (codified there at various levels of detail), either to build up support for their side, or after being defeated to save their crown. In 1093 William II Rufus issued a charter proclaiming freedom of the people (although its text does not survive). His brother and enemy Henry I issued the Charter of Liberties on his coronation in 1100. A century on, the barons raised a rebellion against John I with a demand that he

*When King John was first shown the demands of his nobles that would eventually take final form as the Magna Carta he angrily rejected it as a serious constraint on his freedom to act as he saw fit, above the law if necessary. It took a prolonged period of rebellion and civil war before John was forced to agree the Magna Carta in 1215.*

confirms to the Charter of Henry I. On their victory, King John issued what became the most famous constitutional act of English history: the Magna Carta Libertatum Regni, i.e. the Great Charter of Liberties of the Realm, sealed in the meadow of Runnymede on 15th June 1215.

A summary of its most important constitutional clauses (many others concern property and civil law) is this:

[1] *'the English church shall be free, and shall have her rights entire, and her liberties inviolate'*

[12] *'No scutage nor aid (taxes) shall be imposed on our kingdom, unless by common counsel of our kingdom'*

[13] *'And the city of London shall have all its ancient liberties and free customs, as well by land as by water; furthermore, we decree and grant that all other cities, boroughs, towns, and ports shall have all their liberties and free customs.'*

[20-21] Noone can be *'amerced' (punished)* for an offence *'except by the oath of honest men of the neighbourhood'* and according to the gravity of the offence.

[28-31] *The Crown could not take anyone's 'corn or other provisions' [28], 'horses or carts' [30] or 'wood' [31] against their will and/or 'without immediately tendering money therefor'.*

[39] *'No freeman shall be taken or imprisoned or disseised (wrongfully deprive) or exiled or in any way destroyed, nor will we go upon him nor send upon him, except by the lawful judgment of his peers or by the law of the land.'*

[40] *'To no one will we sell, to no one will we refuse or delay, right or justice.'*

[45] *'We will appoint as justices, constables, sheriffs, or bailiffs only such as know the law of the realm and mean to observe it well.'*

[60] *'Moreover, all these aforesaid customs and liberties, the observance of which we have granted in our kingdom as far as pertains to us toward our men, shall be observed by all of our kingdom, as well clergy as laymen, as far as pertains to them toward their men.'*

[61] *The right to a lawful rebellion was included. Under this provision 25 Barons could choose four of their number to "observe*

*King Edward I seated in Parliament. The first Parliament in anything resembling its modern form was held under Edward's father, Henry III, but it was Edward who made Parliament into a regular feature of the English constitution.*

*and hold... the peace and liberties we have granted and confirmed to them by this our present Charter". Although repealed by King John shortly after signing Magna Carta this provision recognised the right of lawful rebellion against unconstitutional government almost six hundred years before the US Declaration of Independence did the same.*

Magna Carta concludes this provision with the King undertaking the following: "And we shall procure nothing from any one, directly or indirectly, whereby any part of these concessions and liberties might be revoked or diminished; and if any such thing has been procured, let it be void and null, and we shall never use it personally or by another."

What makes Magna Carta 1215 so special? From the constitutional point of view, the Charter itself is no more than simply a Statute, i. e. an Act of the sovereign King made by and with advice and consent of all the estates of the realm. Furthermore, Magna Carta 1215 was one in a long series of almost identical Charters, issued and re-issued by successive Kings in longer or shorter versions over three centuries following the Conquest:

- William II's Charter 1093
- Henry I's Coronation Charter / Charter of Liberties 1100 (14 clauses)
- John I's 'Runnymede Charter' / Magna Carta 1215 (61 clauses)
- Henry III's Magna Carta 1216 (42 clauses) -
- Henry III's Magna Carta 1217 (47 clauses)
- Henry III's Magna Carta 1225 (37 clauses)
- Henry III's Carta Parva 1237 (37 clauses)
- Edward I's Confirmatio Chartarum 1295
- Edward I's statute - Magna Carta 1297…
- Etc.,etc…

According to Sir Edward Coke, Magna Carta was re-confirmed at least 32 times in total, the last one being in 1423 in the reign of Henry VI. Some constitutional historians have suggested it may have been as many as 45 times.

What, then, is so special about Magna Carta 1215? One obvious reason is the epic romanticism of the right to a lawful rebellion, which wrung the Runnymede Charter from the unwilling King, and which is enshrined in the text of that Charter but not in any other version.

Among the national symbols of England, Runnymede certainly ranks equal with Camelot and Trafalgar; but that does not in itself explain the paramount legal force attached to Magna Carta 1215 in our constitutional tradition. In particular historic circumstances it was granted truly "by and with advice and consent of the Lords Spiritual and Temporal, and the Commons" – something later recognised as placing an Act at the top of the constitutional hierarchy.

For a similar reason, Magna Carta 1297 made by Edward I in a formal Parliament, is the version that opens the statute books of today as the earliest statute still in force. Yet, neither the 1215 Charter nor the Charter of 1297 was the first statute in our legal history, and there is no doubt that the legal strength of Magna Carta flows not merely from its being kind of an Act of Parliament.

What makes it so special are its contents. Compared to earlier and later  versions, Magna Carta 1215 is simply the fullest version. It is significant not as an enactment, not as an innovation, but as a code of constitutional rights and liberties which had existed in Common Law long before its time. Why else would each King confirm and re-issue the same statute over and over again in identical language? A statute, once made, remains in force forever, unless repealed. As legislation, a repeated Charter would make no sense. It only made sense as the King's solemn promise to uphold the ancient common law liberties. In Edward I's Confirmatio Chartarum 25. E. I, the High Court of Parliament held that that the Magna Carta should be taken as part of the Common Law, and that any judgement contrary to it is void. (Coke, Institutes, vol. 2; Blackstone, Commentaries, vol. 1, p. 128)

A comparison of Magna Carta 1215 with its previous and shorter version - Charter of Liberties 1100 – is particularly revealing. Putting aside differences resulting from politics of the day (e.g. clauses on amnesty to rebels etc.), the first half of the Magna Carta duplicates the Charter of Liberties almost word for word. Below that, we find a few dozens of detailed clauses in Magna Carta 1215, and in the Charter of Liberties 1100 just one sentence in their place: 'I restore to you the law of King Edward with those amendments introduced into it by my father with the advice of his barons.' A natural and almost inevitable conclusion is that John I's barons, who had started a civil war for a restoration of the Charter of Liberties in the first place, simply endeavoured to codify 'the law of King Edward' and add it to the Magna Carta.

The text of Magna Carta itself suggests that it was by no means an innovation; rather, it was meant as a new code of the old law. It is the brightest example of what Blackstone calls a declaratory statute, made "where the old custom of the kingdom is almost fallen into disuse, or become disputable; in which case the parliament has thought proper, in perpetuum rei testimonium, and for avoiding all doubts and difficulties, to declare what the common law is and ever hath been."

No name stands higher in the history of common law than that of Sir Edward Coke. As Attorney-General, he prosecuted the Gunpowder plot; then as Lord Chief Justice, gave some of the most important constitutional judgements in our history. It was Coke CJ who ruled that the King may not adjudicate cases without judges (Prohibitions del Roy), that the Crown may not legislate without Parliament (The Case of Proclamations), and that even the Parliament may not legislate "against common right and reason" (Dr. Bonham's Case).

It was Coke who first formulated the legal doctrine that "there is no guilty act without a guilty mind", meaning that nobody can be convicted before a certain form of 'malice' – i. e. intent, recklessness, or negligence – is proven. Obviously, modern legislation on 'strict liablity' for some offences, e.g. in the non-payment of the TV license, speeding offences etc., is plainly incompatible with this fundamental doctrine. On this account, his name would have been cursed daily by prosecutors around the world to the day, if only they were better educated. It was quite often cursed by James I and his famous minister, Sir Francis Bacon, who eventually removed him from the judicial bench. Coke then became prominent in the House of Commons; he was the one who drafted the Petition of Right and helped make it become law. He towered over the political and religious controversies of the 17th century with impartial firmness of the finest common law judge, without fear or favour, affection or ill will towards any of the rival parties, giving judgements against the King as often as against the Parliament; neither could count on his loyalty, except to the law.

It was Coke who first said that a man's home is his castle (Institutes, vol. 1, p. 162; Semayne's Case (1604) 77 Eng. Rep. 194, 195; 5 Co. Rep. 91, 195 (K.B.)) and that Magna Carta is such a fellow that he will have no sovereign (House of Commons debate, 17 May 1628). He is one of the very few authors whose treatises, by tradition, may be quoted as common law authorities, without reference to specific cases – it is assumed that these authors knew the common law so well that their word is good enough as an authority. But the common law tradition pays to Coke especially a still higher and unique honour. According to Mr. Justice Blackstone, Coke's writings can be quoted in court without citing the author's name *(Commentaries, Vol. 1, ch.*

*3.3.).* It was apparently assumed in Blackstone's times that any English lawyer must know the four volumes of Coke's Institutes and the thirteen volumes of Reports by heart. Of course, nine out of ten modern QCs have hardly heard of him (or Blackstone, for this matter).

It was Coke who, two centuries after the last confirmation of Magna Carta, in the fifteenth century dug out the ancient statute, then almost forgotten, and insisted on it being the solution to the constitutional controversies of the Stuart era. He wrote a chapter-by-chapter commentary on Magna Carta on the basis of the cases where it was applied (Institutes, vol. 2), where he proved that it was still in force and that "this Charter is declaratory of the ancient Law and Liberty of England, and therefore no new freedom is hereby granted... but a restitution of such as lawfully they had before, and to free them of that which had been usurped and encroached upon them by any power whatsoever".

The result of Coke's campaign for Magna Carta was the Petition of Right 1628. Petition of the Commons was an ancient form of statute from the early history of Parliament, which had long fallen into disuse by that time. Instead of the standard form 'Be it Enacted by the King's Most Excellent Majesty, etc.', a petition was a kind of Bill which originated from the Subjects, and whose purpose was redress of grievances rather than enactment of legislation. The assent of the King, Lords, and Commons gave it the force of a statute, but the form stressed the essentially judicial nature of the Parliament's decision:

*To the King's Most Excellent Majesty,*

*Humbly show unto our Sovereign Lord the King, the Lords Spiritual and Temporal, and Commons in Parliament assembled, that whereas...*

Then follows the list of grievances, always pointing out it was in breach of specified provisions of Magna Carta or a number of other statutes:

*[I-II] Taxation without consent (in various forms);*
*[III-V] Arbitrary imprisonments by orders of the King in Council;*
*[VI] People were compelled to provide lodging to soldiers in their houses.*

*[VII-VIII] Appointed commissioners tried and convicted soldiers and their civilian accomplices under "such summary course and order as is agreeable to martial law", contrary to Magna Carta (i.e. without a judgement of their peers or by common law trial); [IX] Ordinary common law courts refused to accept cases which were supposed to come within such 'martial law' jurisdiction.*

*[X]. They do therefore humbly pray your most excellent Majesty, that no man hereafter be compelled to make or yield any gift, loan, benevolence, tax, or such like charge, without common consent by act of parliament; and that none be called to make answer, or take such oath, or to give attendance, or be confined, or otherwise molested or disquieted concerning the same or for refusal thereof; and that no freeman, in any such manner as is before mentioned, be imprisoned or detained; and that your Majesty would be pleased to remove the said soldiers and mariners, and that your people may not be so burdened in time to come; and that the aforesaid commissions, for proceeding by martial law, may be revoked and annulled; and that hereafter no commissions of like nature may issue forth to any person or persons whatsoever to be executed as aforesaid, lest by color of them any of your Majesty's subjects be destroyed or put to death contrary to the laws and franchise of the land.*

*[XI]. All which they most humbly pray of your most excellent Majesty as their rights and liberties, according to the laws and statutes of this realm; and that your Majesty would also vouchsafe to declare, that the awards, doings, and proceedings, to the prejudice of your people in any of the premises, shall not be drawn hereafter into consequence or example; and that your Majesty would be also graciously pleased, for the further comfort and safety of your people, to declare your royal will and pleasure, that in the things aforesaid all your officers and ministers shall serve you according to the laws and statutes of this realm, as they tender the honor of your Majesty, and the prosperity of this kingdom.*

Once Charles I gave Royal Assent to the Petition of Right, Sir

*On 4 January 1642 King Charles I marched into Parliament with a force of armed soldiers to arrest five MPs on charges of high treason. The Speaker, William Lenthal refused to say where the men were and Charles left. The English Civil War between King and Parliament began soon after. Never since has any monarch entered Parliament without permission.*

Edward Coke's quarrel with the Crown was over. He became a royalist as loyal as any until his death in 1634.

But the conflict went on, and it took over another half a century of revolutions and restorations until it was quite settled. The last of the great declaratory statutes of our Constitution is known as the Bill of Rights 1689. Like its predecessors, the Bill of Rights begins by describing abuses, and then proceeds to declare the actual rights:

*...And thereupon the said Lords Spiritual and Temporal and Commons... do in the first place (as their ancestors in like case have usually done) for the vindicating and asserting their ancient rights and liberties declare*

*That the pretended power of suspending the laws or the execution of laws by regal authority without consent of Parliament is illegal;*

*That the pretended power of dispensing with laws or the execution of laws by regal authority, as it hath been assumed and exercised of late, is illegal;*

*That the commission for erecting the late Court of Commissioners for Ecclesiastical Causes, and all other commissions and courts of like nature, are illegal and pernicious;*

*That levying money for or to the use of the Crown by pretence of prerogative, without grant of Parliament, for longer time, or in other manner than the same is or shall be granted, is illegal;*

*That it is the right of the subjects to petition the king, and all commitments and prosecutions for such petitioning are illegal;*

*That the raising or keeping a standing army within the kingdom in time of peace, unless it be with consent of Parliament, is against law;*

*That the subjects which are Protestants may have arms for their defence suitable to their conditions and as allowed by law;*

*That election of members of Parliament ought to be free;*

*That the freedom of speech and debates or proceedings in Parliament ought not to be impeached or questioned in any court or place out of Parliament;*

*That excessive bail ought not to be required, nor excessive fines imposed, nor cruel and unusual punishments inflicted;*

*That jurors ought to be duly impanelled and returned, and jurors which pass upon men in trials for high treason ought to be freeholders;*

*That all grants and promises of fines and forfeitures of particular persons before conviction are illegal and void;*

*And that for redress of all grievances, and for the amending, strengthening and preserving of the laws, Parliaments ought to be held frequently.*

*And they do claim, demand and insist upon all and singular the premises as their undoubted rights and liberties, and that no declarations, judgments, doings or proceedings to the prejudice of the people in any of the said premises ought in any wise to be drawn hereafter into consequence or example...*

## LEX LEGUM AND PASSING CONVENTIONS

Magna Carta is such a fellow that he will have no sovereign. There is a part of our law which cannot be changed at all, which cannot be changed by Parliament, by a conquest, by a revolution, by a unanimous consent of the whole country. In the old books, that part of the law was called the Law of Reason, the Law of Nature, or the Law of God; I shall denote it here by an equally ancient but philosophically neutral name lex legum, the "law of laws".

i)        No Act of Parliament, and nothing on earth, can legally make someone a judge in his own case:

- Dr Bonham's Case (1610) 8 Co Rep 114a per Coke CJ;
- Day v Savadge (1614) Hob 85; 80 ER 235 per Hobart CJ.
- R. v Love (1653) 5 State Tr 825
- City of London v. Wood (1702), per Holt CJ

*The series of constitutional crises that began with King Charles I's dispute with Parliament ended when Queen Mary II and her husband King William III accepted the Bill of Rights and other legislation that was enacted as a result of the Glorious Revolution of 1688.*

ii)     No Act of Parliament, and nothing on earth, can make the court "to condemn the innocent and condemn the guilty", or to punish someone for an offence they did not commit:

Lord Cromwell's Case (1581) 4 Co Rep. 12b

iii)     No Act of Parliament, and nothing on earth, can take away the royal power to pardon convicted criminals:

Case of Non Obstante, or Dispensing Power, 12 Co Rep 18, per Coke LJ.

The examples are countless. What is most important for us is that, both on ancient and modern authorities, the constitutional fundamentals such as the rule of law, sovereignty, government by consent are also part of the lex legum.

iv)     The subject's allegiance to his sovereign is "a law of nature", which is "immutable" and "cannot be changed":

Calvin's Case (1608) 7 Coke Reports 2a

v)     The Queen in Parliament cannot abolish her own sovereignty. "Thus there is nothing in the 1972 [European Communities] Act which allows the Court of Justice, or any other institutions of the EU, to touch or qualify the conditions of Parliament's legislative supremacy in the United Kingdom. Not because the legislature chose not to allow it; because by our law it could not allow it. That being so, the legislative and judicial institutions of the EU cannot intrude upon those conditions. The British Parliament has not the authority to authorise any such thing. Being sovereign, it cannot abandon its sovereignty." -

Metric Martyrs (Thoburn v Sunderland City Council) [2002] EWHC 195 (Admin) [2003] Q.B. 151, per Laws LJ and Crane J

vi)     Both Magna Carta and the Bill of Rights assert they should remain the law of the land forever, and any statute purporting to repeal or override them has no effect. Dicean jurisprudence ignores the common law doctrine of lex legum, and dismisses those 'entrenchment' provisions as a Parliament's vain attempts to bind its successors. In fact, they are not. Magna Carta and Bill of Rights are declaratory statutes; they declare the common law as it is and has always been, and their peculiarity is that they declare the part of the common law which is immutable and cannot be changed. This is not the Parliament that binds its successors here - it is the common law that binds Parliament.

This is a strictly legal view of the Constitution and the Common Law even if it is not the conventional view among many in modern politics. For the foolish theory of parliamentary omnipotence is no part of the common law. An Act of Parliament may consist of a meaningless text incapable of being law; it may contradict itself; it may be intended solely to bind its successors. Of course, such a statute would be void – at least in part. A statute abolishing the Constitution would be void – for it is only the Constitution that gives any force to any statute in the first place.

The English Constitution is often praised for being 'flexible'. This is true enough; but it is often misunderstood what flexibility means. It certainly does not mean (as is often asserted) that any part of it can be easily changed by a mere Act of Parliament. Flexibility does not mean thorough fragility. Rather, it means a combination of a solid core with pliable margins; and that is what our Constitution has. Its first principles are enshrined in the immutable lex legum; but all further details are regulated by mutable statutes (e.g. setting out an electoral system) or even unwritten conventions.

The secret of its flexibility is in separation of law from politics: the core principles are purely legal, and the politics is brushed to the margins. This is where many foreign imitations of a constitution have failed, by placing such things as equality and fraternity before such things as rule of law. This is the great discovery of England, which has amazed and annoyed it neighbours for many centuries. To make the rule of law complete, the relations between the state and its subjects must also be based upon legal, and not political, principles. And this is where this peculiar idea of a constitution comes from.

At the margins of our constitution, conventions are flexible enough, whether or not they are codified in statutes; and conventions may be influenced by changing political circumstances. Matters regulated entirely by unwritten conventions include, for example, the existence and powers of the Cabinet, the appointment of its members, the office and powers of the Prime Minister, the government's obligations arising from electoral manifestos, the government's responsibility to the Parliament and the Parliament's responsibility to the electorate. In brief, it is nearly the entire façade of our Constitution. But it would be a sore misunderstanding to mistake this façade for the basis.

The constitutional convention has been difficult to define, and the only existing definition is rather vague. To establish whether a practice amounts to a convention, Sir Ivor Jenning writes, three questions should be asked:

"Firstly, are there any precedents for the convention?

"Secondly, did the actors believe they were bound by a rule? and;

"Finally, is there a reason for the rule?

"A single precedent with a good reason may be enough to establish the rule. A whole string of precedents without such a reason will be of no avail, unless it is perfectly certain that the persons concerned regarded them as bound by it."

Of course, what may be considered a 'good reason' would change with time, and be affected by the politics of the day, so the conventions change, too. There is nothing unlawful about a constitutional reform. But having drawn a clear distinction between the legal core of the Constitution and its marginal political conventions, we can also easily distinguish between a bona fide reform and a treasonous subversion of the Constitution.

A genuine reformer may change conventions, if there is a good reason; but he will keep the lex legum sacred. A traitor would seek to 'reform' the very principles of Sovereignty, Government by Consent, Rule of Law; to repeal parts of whole of Magna Carta, Petition of Rights, or the Bill of Rights. Such an attempt would be unlawful, for there is no legitimate power on earth that can change any of these things. The true constitution would still be there – but only as a legal fiction. As a matter of fact, we would be put in an illegally constituted state.

# PART II. REVOLUTION

### THE FALL OF PARLIAMENT

Perhaps the most basic and commonplace lesson of history is that democracy is mortal. Once born, it is never secure. It can be killed. Moreover, it is very typical of formal democratic institutions to survive for a long time while the democracy itself is long dead. The Roman Senate and the Roman forum long outlived the Roman Republic. Henry VIII ruled Britain with a very acquiescent parliamentary majority.

The Reichstag had its perfectly comfortable place in Nazi Germany. Today, it may be argued that we are not quite there yet; but there is no doubt that we are moving in that direction. So His Lordship, Baron of Foy in the County of Herefordshire and of Hartlepool in the County of Durham, alias Peter Mandelson, may be quite right in saying that we live in a "post-democratic age". But if democracy is dead, this has been a suspicious death. We need some kind of coroner's inquest to know its causes.

Having now recalled the fundamentals of our Constitution, it hardly requires any proof that the history of the past 40 years has been a history of its destruction. This fact cannot be denied; it can only be concealed. And so it was, for the time being.

But the usurpation of our sovereignty by the EU and its quislings is a sore result of a much larger and longer constitutional crisis, caused by the advances of 19th century academic lunacies such as socialism, utilitarianism, and legal positivism. That crisis still goes on; and in a sense, it is more profound than any similar crisis known to our history. In the past revolutions and civil wars – be it in the 17th, 13th, or 11th century – the ancient common law was the ultimate point of reference.

Each side in all those conflicts claimed to defend the old constitution and denounced its opponents as innovators. In those times, it was typical to oppose a reform solely on the grounds that it is an 'innovation' – that word could become a death sentence to any parliamentary bill. The 'reform' was understood only as making the ancient principles work, as removing any factors which frustrate or deform the old system; restoration, as opposed to innovation. The idea of law being updated to reflect the changing circumstances was unthinkable. It was for the realities to be brought in line with the law.

The modern attitude is the very opposite of that. In contemporary politics, each party claims to be 'progressive' and denounces its opponents as 'reactionary'. The faith in the tradition is gone; the new point of reference is the faith in progressive innovations. The old Parliaments were courts where political rivals tested whose claim to power was more lawful. Parliament has ended up in the most lawless role you could imagine for it – as a kind of a Supreme Soviet, nominally sovereign, effectively powerless, tirelessly rubber-stamping decrees for the utmost destruction of the Constitution.

This is where it ends; but this in not where it began. It began when the Parliament claimed omnipotence to legislate for the greatest happiness of the greatest number; when it remembered that it could be under no man, but forgot that it was under God and the law. Having placed itself above God and the law, it now finds itself under many strange men – who operate out of Brussels and Strasbourg.

There was a time when this country would revolt against any king who 'abolished old laws and every year passed new ones'. Yet in modern times, it is supposed to be a respectable duty of Parliament to do that every day. It abolishes old laws and passes new ones in a mad rush; it is so busy with that that it can no longer even justify its name as a talking shop.

Parliament was meant as a place of debate, and in the previous centuries, there were debates worth listening to. Nowadays, the Parliament is in such a hurry to legislate that it had to impose severe restrictions on the freedom of speech for its own members, the tightest possible timetables and deadlines, to abolish and enact enough laws in time. Yet it cannot cope, so most of that work has to be delegated to elsewhere, while the Parliament is left with frantic rubber-stamping.

It is a fact that over 80 per cent of the legislation is now made by the EU. In an article for the newspaper Welt am Sonntag in January 2007, former German President Roman Hertzog said that 84% of German laws stemmed from the EU. We shall come to that; but out of the remaining 20 per cent, how much is actually made by the elected Parliament? A lot of it are statutory instruments, regulations and orders made by Ministers – essentially non-parliamentary legislation, which was condemned as unconstitutional in the Case of Proclamations. What is left for proper Acts of Parliament are only a small section; but it is still an avalanche of paper which the Parliament can only just rubber-stamp but cannot properly consider. In fact, it has been made elsewhere.

Thus there is a little known and entirely unaccountable body called the Law Commission which, for a number of decades now, is systematically working on the so-called 'law reform' or 'law revision'. It goes through every area of common law and statute law, and recommends very substantial changes to 'modernise' it, which are usually accepted on the nod. All it says in its reports is that such and such laws have become 'obsolete' and would better be repealed, and the rest would better be codified in a single statute, with such and such changes; in that form, the law would become much more convenient for the lawyers. And even if the Members of Parliament cared about the law, even if they had time to look into all this, anyhow they lack the expertise to argue against professional lawyers. As it is, they just go on rubber-stamping.

Do you know that:

• Most of the Magna Carta has by now been repealed, with the exception of but four articles?

• Trial by jury only survives as a medieval relic with 98 per cent of all criminal cases being decided by magistrates at something officially called 'summary trials'?

• The right of habeas corpus has been abolished for anyone who has the misfortune to be named in a European Arrest Warrant?

How many people in this country have consciously voted for any of these things? And if any of these things could be done without a popular mandate, this is a final, impartial proof that the age of democracy is over.

We have gone a full circle. The Crown in Parliament is, once more, merely a more pompous version of the Crown. And the Crown is effectively usurped by its evil counsellors. As we are approaching the 800th anniversary of the Magna Carta, we suddenly discover that we are back to square one.

Now, imagine that some really evil counsellors, some criminals or traitors (to keep the example abstract, let them be secret agents of Taliban) have somehow crawled into the position of Ministers of the Crown. It is not too difficult these days – you only have to perform well on television and to have no moral scruples. Obviously, these people would want to get rid of a number of laws which safeguard the democracy against such subversive plans as theirs. They will find this very easy these days. They will find there a perpetually working shredding machine for repealing 'obsolete' laws, a dozen per day. What can be easier for them than to slip the vital safeguards of democracy into the waste heap?

The whole point of a Constitution is to protect the country against the potentialities of an evil or stupid government. I do think there have been and are traitors in the government; but whether I am right or wrong, it is a fact that some day there might be traitors in the government, and the Constitution would be defenceless against them. For this matter, in present circumstances it can be unconsciously destroyed by well-meaning idiots just as by conscious criminals.

By an extraordinary coincidence, all the Statutes of Praemunire (with one notable exception, of which more later) were repealed as 'obsolete' in 1967, followed by a similar repeal of the Act of Supremacy in 1969. After several centuries The Law Commission had suddenly noticed the 'obsolescence' of those constitutional statutes precisely at the time when the idea of our joining the EEC was being seriously considered in government circles. By an even more of a coincidence, one of the first bills introduced by the Blair government in 1998 repealed Treason Act 1795 and abolished the death penalty for high treason (Crime and Disorder Act 1998, S. 36).

## THE EU'S 'NEW LEGAL ORDER'

Today, it hardly requires any proof that this country's membership of the EU is in every respect incompatible with Sovereignty of the Queen in Parliament. As such, it is unconstitutional. Throughout its history, the European Community/Union has had its own system of constitutional law, entirely alien to ours. The EU law is governed by the provisions of EU Treaties, which rank above any other provisions of national or international law within the EU. The Treaties create the EU's own sovereign legislature in the form of Commission, Council and Parliament (a very rough parody of, respectively, the Crown, the Lords and the Commons in English Constitution). EU legislation falls into two main categories:

1. Regulations, which must be automatically enforced as law throughout the EU, overriding any national law, Parliament having already surrendered power in the relevant legislative areas.

2. Directives and Decisions, which are supposed to bind our own Parliament (and other parliaments of member-states) to legislate in a prescribed way – effectively simply to rubber-stamp the EU law as national law. Parliament may debate them as much as they like but they have no choice but to transpose them into national law.

It is by these means that the EU now makes over 80 per cent of all new laws in this country.

Further, the EU has its own European Court of Justice in Luxembourg, whose decisions are also binding on our Parliament, government, courts, and the population. Furthermore, our courts are obliged to refer cases to Luxemburg wherever a question of 'EU law' is involved.

The EU asserts (and our Parliament and courts have accepted) the undisputed principles of 'supremacy' and 'direct effect' of the 'EU law' throughout the EU. The European Constitution 2005 declared them in so many words; but they had been established from the very early days of the Community.

Indeed, from its very beginning, the EEC claimed 'sovereignty' over the member-states in so many words. In its early constitutional judgements, most famously in Costa v ENEL (1964) , the European

Court of Justice held:

> *By contrast with ordinary international treaties, the EEC Treaty has created its own legal system which, on the entry into force of the Treaty, became an integral part of the legal systems of the Member States and which their courts are bound to apply.*

By creating a Community of unlimited duration, having its own institutions, its own personality, its own legal capacity and capacity of representation on the international plane and, more particularly, real powers stemming from a limitation of sovereignty or a transfer of powers from the States to the Community, the Member States have limited their sovereign rights, albeit within limited fields, and have thus created a body of law which binds both their nationals and themselves.

So, the EU has created its own constitution and asserted its sovereignty from the very beginning, long before anyone dared to openly call it a Constitution. For the first time, the European Court of Justice described the EEC Treaty as its 'basic constitutional charter' in the case of Partie Ecologiste 'Les Verts' v. Parliament (1986). It was only twenty years later that the EU dared to utter the word 'constitution' aloud; and from that it was forced to retreat. But in truth, the moment the EU constitution was established, albeit discretely, was the Treaty of Rome 1957.

Today, it is no longer concealed or denied that the real goal of the EEC/EU is, and has always been, a single European state; and it has been a deliberate tactics to keep the final goal secret. The deceivers themselves have now admitted the 'great deception'. But at the time, anybody who suggested there may be more to the Common Market than simply a common market, that it may be only the first slice cut in a salami tactics of Euro-federalism, was ridiculed as a conspiracy theorist. Now it turns out to have been a salami tactics after all.

One might wonder even half a century ago why one needed any supra-national organisation to have a customs union, while all other customs unions in history functioned perfectly well without any organisations, parliaments or courts. Such questions were asked at the time, and silenced. So the new constitutional principle was accepted as something minor and insignificant. Of course, we knew – or if we did not know, we felt with our bones – that a constitutional principle can never be insignificant. So Edward Heath simply lied that there was no constitutional principle at stake. That story is well-known and evidenced by the archives, so there is no need to recite it here in greater detail.

Once the sovereignty itself was transferred to Brussels, it became merely a technical matter to transfer the actual powers to it slice by slice. At first, we were told that sovereignty was only an abstract concept and transferring it to Brussels would hardly even affect our lives. And then, the gradual transfer of actual powers was justified as a mere extension of a well-established and working principle.

But that was another lie. In fact, each and every EEC/EU treaty was another and separate treason.

By now, it is fairly obvious that the United Kingdom's membership in any such 'new legal order' is legally impossible, because a country cannot live under two different constitutions. The EU constitution is manifestly incompatible with the basic principle of ours: the Sovereignty of the Queen in Parliament. In particular:

-        It creates another legislature to rival the Queen in Parliament, and expressly makes the EU legislation supreme over the Acts of Parliament;

-        Likewise, it enables legislation other than Acts of Parliament to prevail over the Common Law, which is equally unconstitutional (see, for example, the Case of Proclamations);

-        It binds the Parliament to legislate as prescribed in the EU directives, and not to legislate in contravention to 'EU law'. As we remember, it is essential to Sovereignty that the Parliament can never be so bound; even the Parliament itself cannot bind its successors.

-        By EU legislation, the law of England can now be made, unmade, or altered manifestly without the consent of the subjects. Opponents will argue that it is enacted by democratic will of the European Parliament; but all UK MEPs together only amount to 8 per cent of the total, and any meaningful notion of national democracy is defunct.

- Any step towards subjecting England to this 'new legal order' is criminal – it is Praemunire by definition, viz. "introducing a foreign power into the land, and creating imperium in imperio" .

- In particular, a classic instance of Praemunire is to assert, expressly or implicitly, that England is subject to jurisdiction of any foreign court. This clearly applies to the European Court of Justice as much as it applied to the courts of the Roman Church. As explained above, although the offence of Praemunire is now abolished, its underlying constitutional principle survives in the common law.

- Likewise, any Cabinet Minister or Privy Counsellor who takes or contemplates any steps towards subjecting England to the 'new legal order' is in breach of the Privy Council oath of allegiance, i. e. to "assist and defend all Jurisdictions, Pre-eminences, and Authorities, granted to Her Majesty, and annexed to the Crown… against all Foreign Princes, Persons, Prelates, States, or Potentates" and thus guilty of high treason.

Such constitutional objections to signing any of the EU Treaties were, indeed, obvious from a very early stage. In 1971 Raymond Blackburn applied to the High Court for a declaration that provisions of the Treaty of Rome purporting to limit Sovereignty of the Queen in Parliament were void (Blackburn v Attorney-General). The action failed both in High Court and then in Court of Appeal because the courts had no jurisdiction to adjudicate on international treaties, especially before they were signed. Even after the treaty is signed, it does not become law until and unless the Parliament enacts a statute expressly 'incorporating' its provisions into the law. Only after that, the Court of Appeal held, would it have jurisdiction to consider the constitutional effects of such a statute.

Once the Treaty of Rome was signed, Norris McWhirter applied for a judicial review of the government's decision to sign it (McWhirter v Attorney-General (1972)). Again, the case reached the Court of Appeal. Again, Lord Denning held that the courts had no jurisdiction to interfere with the Royal Prerogative to make treaties. Lord Phillimore added that the Courts take no notice of international treaties; it would be the Act of Parliament ratifying it which "will or will not alter the law of this country; and unless and until that Bill becomes law this Court is not concerned with the provisions of the Treaty".

Similar challenges to the Maastricht Treaty (R v Foreign Secretary, Ex p. Rees-Mogg (1994)), to Nice Treaty (McWhirter v Foreign Secretary (2003)) and to the European Constitution (R. v. Foreign Secretary, Ex p. Southall (2003)) were rejected on the same grounds. Treaties were no laws in themselves, so they were for the Crown and not for the Courts. And then, whether they should be 'incorporated' into the law, was for the Parliament and not for the Courts.

## EU CITIZENSHIP AND THE ABOLITION OF MONARCHY

Perhaps the most obviously unconstitutional element of the EU's 'legal order' is the so-called 'EU citizenship', which has been imposed on each of us without our consent. No longer the Queen's subjects, we are now supposed to be citizens of the European Union, and as such, to "be subject to the duties provided for in the Treaties" (Article 20 of the Treaty on the Functioning of the EU).

From the constitutional point of view, 'a citizen' is synonymous to 'a subject'. As explained above, the legal relations of protection and allegiance between the Sovereign and Subject are so fundamental, that in Calvin's Case they were held to be "due by the law of nature". The case was, if we translate it into modern terms, all about citizenship – about property rights of a Scottish subject in England, and whether they were different from the rights of an English subject.

Since the Queen is the Guardian of the Constitution and the living symbol of it, and indeed our entire monarchy has developed into a safeguard of the Constitution, the ancient doctrine remained perfectly adequate in the modern world. As Queen's subjects, we owed allegiance to Her Majesty and were entitled to her protection. In legal terms, this meant, first and foremost, allegiance to the Constitution and protection by the Constitution.

In 1983, the Tory government introduced a 'modernisation' of the system, making all of us 'UK citizens' rather than subjects. The Queen was made a 'citizen', too. Although rather tasteless, the reform seemed legally meaningless and constitutionally harmless – unless you read the small print of the EU Treaties, whereby every 'citizen' of every member-state is automatically made a citizen of the EU and "shall enjoy the rights and be subject to the duties provided for in the Treaties". Translating this back into the English constitutional language, this makes us subjects of a sovereign other than ours.

It is, of course, illegal for the government to make us citizens of somewhere else without our consent. That is why, for example, when our former colonies formed the United States of America, they could not impose the US citizenship on the population without their consent.

*Edward Heath took Britain into the European Economic Community in 1973 without the democratic mandate to do so and on the basis of lies and deceit. His actions proved to have massive repercussions for the Constitution of England and the survival of England as an independent nation state.*

Everyone was given a choice of either remaining a subject of the English King or becoming a US citizen. So the consent was obtained, and the new sovereign-subject relationship legally formed. Without such consent, our 'EU citizenship' remains fundamentally unlawful.

Furthermore, the Queen herself has also been made a citizen of the EU. Under the English Constitution, this is literally an impossible position: the whole point of a Sovereign is that she is sovereign. By definition, the Queen cannot be anyone's subject or, to put it another way, citizen - and as such, "subject to the duties provided for in the Treaties". Making the Queen an EU citizen effectively means an abolition of monarchy and of sovereignty.

Fortunately, this cannot be done. There is a clear-cut historic and legal precedent for precisely this situation – the case of King John and the Pope, mentioned above. For exactly the same reasons as 800 years ago, the 'EU citizenship' of the Queen is illegal and void. It is not within the legal power of the Queen to make herself a subject (citizen) to the EU, the Pope, anything or anybody. The Crown is not hers to give away – it is only held on trust for her successors. Therefore, the English law simply does not recognise the 'EU citizenship' of the Queen – or, for this matter, of her subjects.

## EUROPEAN COMMUNITIES ACT 1972

Sure enough, in due course the Treaty of Rome was signed, and the Parliament passed The European Communities Act 1972. It incorporates the provisions of the EU law into the English law. A momentous statute, perhaps the most important one our Parliament has ever passed – after all, it pretty nearly introduces a new Constitution for this country. Certainly, the deep legal meaning of these words deserves to be considered carefully, not only by every lawyer, but by every citizen. After defining "the Treaties" as those listed in an attached schedule, the Act (as amended and in force today) provides:

*Section 2 - General implementation of Treaties.*
*(1) All such rights, powers, liabilities, obligations and restrictions from time to time created or arising by or under the Treaties, and*

*all such remedies and procedures from time to time provided for by or under the Treaties, as in accordance with the Treaties are without further enactment to be given legal effect or used in the United Kingdom shall be recognised and available in law, and be enforced, allowed and followed accordingly; and the expression "enforceable EU right" and similar expressions shall be read as referring to one to which this subsection applies.*

*(2) Subject to Schedule 2 to this Act, at any time after its passing Her Majesty may by Order in Council, and any designated Minister or department may by order, rules, regulations or scheme, make provision —*

*(a) for the purpose of implementing any EU obligation of the United Kingdom, or enabling any such obligation to be implemented, or of enabling any rights enjoyed or to be enjoyed by the United Kingdom under or by virtue of the Treaties to be exercised; or*

*(b) for the purpose of dealing with matters arising out of or related to any such obligation or rights or the coming into force, or the operation from time to time, of subsection (1) above; and in the exercise of any statutory power or duty, including any power to give directions or to legislate by means of orders, rules, regulations or other subordinate instrument, the person entrusted with the power or duty may have regard to the objects of the EU and to any such obligation or rights as aforesaid.*

*In this subsection "designated Minister or department" means such Minister of the Crown or government department as may from time to time be designated by Order in Council in relation to any matter or for any purpose, but subject to such restrictions or conditions (if any) as may be specified by the Order in Council. [...]*

*(4) The provision that may be made under subsection (2) above includes, subject to Schedule 2 to this Act, any such provision (of any such extent) as might be made by Act of Parliament, and any enactment passed or to be passed, other than one contained in this part of this Act, shall be construed and have effect subject to*

> *the foregoing provisions of this section; but, except as may be provided by any Act passed after this Act, Schedule 2 shall have effect in connection with the powers conferred by this and the following sections of this Act to make Orders in Council or orders, rules, regulations or schemes.*

These incomprehensible words of the great statute are placed at the pinnacle of the splendid palace of our modernised constitution. These words are, of necessity, written in flaming gold across the mind of every judge or magistrate; for they are the supreme law of this kingdom which protects the freedom and justice for all its subjects. One is surprised they are not yet inscribed in huge letters over the façade of every court of law and every government building. After all, even if our lawyers and statesmen no longer respect such things as Magna Carta, every responsible lawyer or statesman needs at least some Constitution to celebrate.

On frequent occasions when a legal text sounds to me like meaningless mumbo-jumbo I, being a modest layman, tend to blame my own ignorance. I assume it actually does mean something that is simply beyond my learning. So, as a modest layman should, I asked lawyers to explain to me the meaning of Section 2 of the European Communities Act 1972.

The answer (given by honest lawyers off the record) is this: it is indeed pseudo-legal gibberish. Hardly anybody, including our greatest lawyers and top judges, understand what it means. They simply try to sail in those muddied waters as best they can, on the vague general assumption that somehow this language does incorporate the 'EU law' into the English law and makes it supreme.

So, here we have a statute of enormous constitutional importance, overturning most fundamental principles of the English Constitution, introducing a whole body of entirely alien law and government into the English law as a supreme and better system. Its effect on every aspect of our lives cannot be exaggerated. If such a statute can be lawfully made at all, one would at least expect some clarity from it. Instead, we have something worse then the smallest print in the most crooked contract in the world.

Of course, the maze of 'EU law' does not end with the European Communities Act 1972. That is only the entrance to the maze – it is just that nobody has ever reached further than there. When you come to the actual treaties, regulations, directives, and legislation implementing those directives, those are further hundreds of thousands of pages of, mostly, pseudo-legal gibberish. And then, for completeness of legal certainty, another dimension is added by the maze of Britain's reservations: 'opt-outs', 'opt-ins', 'opt-outs from opt-ins', 'opt-ins into opt-outs', etc.

All this has created endless confusion in Courts as to what parts of the 'EU law' (even if it can be understood) are or are not 'incorporated' into the English law, in what ways, and to what extent. That confusion continues to this day. Only this year, no lesser legal minds than seven judges of the Supreme Court discovered, in Assange v. Swedish Prosecution Authority, that certain fundamental provisions of EU law are not incorporated into the English law and must be ignored. Unfortunately, this fact had been totally overlooked in earlier decisions of the same elevated Court, the void provisions of EU law were enforced, and thousands of people were unlawfully sent to foreign prisons under European Arrest Warrants. The dissenting opinion of Lord Mance, paras 201-218 of the judgement. Although it is a dissenting opinion, on the particular point discussed here, their other Lordships and Her Ladyship agreed with Lord Mance: see Lord Phillips at para 10, Lord Brown at para 98, Lord Kerr at para 112, Lord Dyson at para 121, Lady Hale at paras 175-176.

## THE METRIC MARTYRS CASE

The High Court has made one desperate attempt to unravel the European Communities Act and to reconcile it with the English Constitution. That was in the case of Thoburn v Sunderland City Council, popularly known as that of The Metric Martyrs (2002). An EU directive, in its infinite wisdom, ordered that all traders in the European Union may only sell vegetables by kilograms and made it criminal to sell them by pounds. The UK government duly rubber-stamped the directive, as it was bound to. Under the European

Communities Act (or rather, under such a vague understanding of it as the best lawyers could master), this meant that the directive became a part of the English law, supreme to any Act of our own Parliament.

At the same time, there was in force The Weights and Measures Act 1985, which stated directly the opposite: that all traders were free to use metric or imperial measures as they pleased. So, several seditious traders continued to weigh things in pounds and were in due course prosecuted as criminals against the EU directive. From the EU viewpoint, this meant a conflict between the EU law and a national law, so, of course, the EU law was supreme.

From an English constitutional viewpoint, this was a conflict between two Acts of the sovereign Parliament: The European Communities Act 1972 and The Weights and Measures Act 1985. Being Acts of Parliament, both have the force of law. The English Constitution is very clear on how such conflicts should be resolved: the later Act always has precedence over the earlier one. This is because the Parliament is sovereign, so 'no Parliament can bind its successors'. The rule is known as the doctrine of 'implied repeal': if the sovereign Parliament has legislated contrary to its earlier statute, it is deemed to have repealed the older contradictory provision. So, under the English Constitution, the English Weights and Measures Act had to trump the EU directive.

As simple as that was the dilemma when it came before the High Court, argued there between two eminent barristers called Mr. Shrimpton and Mrs. Sharpston. The matter was convoluted enough before; but the remarkably clever judgement attempted to reconcile the irreconcilable – and only made things worse.

Lord Justice Laws and Mr Justice Crane held that whatever the European Court of Justice stated in Costa v ENEL and other such cases, under the English Constitution, the sovereignty remained with the Queen in Parliament. The European Communities Act could not, and did not, transfer it to the EU:

"Whatever may be the position elsewhere, the law of England disallows any such assumption. Parliament cannot bind its successors by stipulating against repeal, wholly or partly, of the 1972 Act. It cannot stipulate as to the manner and form of any subsequent legislation. It cannot stipulate against implied repeal any more than it can stipulate against express repeal. Thus there is nothing in the 1972 Act which allows the Court of Justice, or any other institutions of the EU, to touch or qualify the conditions of Parliament's legislative supremacy in the United Kingdom. Not because the legislature chose not to allow it; because by our law it could not allow it.

That being so, the legislative and judicial institutions of the EU cannot intrude upon those conditions. The British Parliament has not the authority to authorise any such thing. Being sovereign, it cannot abandon its sovereignty. Accordingly there are no circumstances in which the jurisprudence of the Court of Justice can elevate Community law to a status within the corpus of English domestic law to which it could not aspire by any route of English law itself."

So far so good; no doubt a robust judge like Sir Edward Coke would have the courage to take this to its logical conclusions, and the judgement would become a death sentence to any 'supremacy' of the 'EU law'. But the judges in that case dared not to do that. Instead, they proposed a complex, controversial and novel constitutional compromise:

1. The Parliament enjoys Sovereignty and cannot abandon it; however it could, and did, delegate certain legislative powers to the EU, and provided that the EU law is 'supreme'.

2. That sovereignty and supremacy are therefore different things. Sovereignty, under the English Constitution, belongs to the UK Parliament; but the supremacy, by force of the European Communities Act, belongs to the EU law.

3. The European Communities Act gave the government a so-called 'Henry VIII power' [i. e. the power to legislate without Parliament, condemned in Case of Proclamations] to amend the Weights and Measures Act (or any other Act of Parliament) as the EU directive demanded.

4. There are two different classes of the Acts of Parliament: 'ordinary' statutes and 'constitutional' statutes. The judgement defines a 'constitutional statute' as a one "which (a) conditions the legal

relationship between citizen and state in some general, overarching manner, or (b) enlarges or diminishes the scope of what we would now regard as fundamental constitutional rights. (a) and (b) are of necessity closely related: it is difficult to think of an instance of (a) that is not also an instance of (b). The special status of constitutional statutes follows the special status of constitutional rights. Examples are Magna Carta 1297 (25 Edw 1), the Bill of Rights 1689 (1 Will & Mary sess 2 c 2), the Union with Scotland Act 1706 (6 Anne c 11), the Reform Acts which distributed and enlarged the franchise ( Representation of the People Acts 1832 (2 & 3 Will 4 c 45), 1867 (30 & 31 Vict c 102) and 1884 (48 & 49 Vict c 3)), the Human Rights Act 1998, the Scotland Act 1998 and the Government of Wales Act 1998 . The 1972 Act clearly belongs in this family."

5. 'Constitutional statutes', from Magna Carta to the European Communities Act, are an exception from the doctrine of implied repeal. Unless repealed expressly, they remain in force, and override any 'ordinary statutes'. Lord Justice Laws added: "In the event, which no doubt would never happen in the real world, that a European measure was seen to be repugnant to a fundamental or constitutional right guaranteed by the law of England, a question would arise whether the general words of the 1972 Act were sufficient to incorporate the measure and give it overriding effect in domestic law. But that is very far from this case."

So the EU directive trumped the UK Act of Parliament after all, and the criminal conviction of 'Metric Martyrs' was upheld. Amidst further appeals, Mr. Thoburn died of a heart attack, which was widely attributed to the stress of persecution.

Many critics have pointed out the obvious truth that the judgement creates more problems than it solves. Sovereignty and Supremacy had always been held to be the same thing in English Constitution; the attempt to split this particular hair struck many lawyers as pure sophistry. It is fundamental in Common law that the sovereign Parliament can have no rival legislature. It is equally fundamental that no Parliament can bind its successors; and a fortiori that nobody else can bind the Parliament. The proposed definition of 'constitutional statutes' is extremely vague. Having first-class and second-class statutes is altogether an innovation with no real basis in the common law. Last not least, the EU itself certainly does not accept any similar hair-splitting on this matter, but brutally asserts its own Sovereignty and Supremacy, which is the same thing.

To put it crudely (and with the greatest respect to their Lordships), the judgement is so clever as to be schizoid. It evidently bends the law to the point of almost breaking it, simply in order to arrive at a specific result - which is the very opposite of what any court is supposed to do.

The final footnote to the judgement of Lord Justice Laws is a perfectly ironic symbol of its entire hair-splitting compromise:

*In the course of the hearing I made no secret of my dismay at the way in which the criminal offences relevant to the first three of these appeals had been created. It is a nightmare of a paper chase. I accept that there was no prejudice to these individual appellants, who knew well what the law was because they were concerned to campaign against it. But, in principle, I regard it as lamentable that criminal offences should be created by such a maze of cross-references in subordinate legislation.*

With respect, if His Lordship allowed himself to think and talk about this more plainly, he would have discovered that anything created by 'EU law' is always a maze of cross-references which begins and ends in the darkness of Section 2 of the European Communities Act; and the defendants could not "know well what the law was" while even the judges never know that with 'EU law'.

## THE RULE OF NONSENSE

From the mind-boggling complexities of such cases as The Metric Martyrs, at least one thing is perfectly clear. The problem begins with sovereignty, but it does not end there. Sovereignty had always been but a fortress protecting the Rule of Law and democracy within it. The enemy has taken its walls and towers; it would be foolish to assume that they were only interested in fortifications, and that the city will remain safe inside. The destruction of sovereignty means the destruction of freedom under the law.

The EU also claims to be governed by the 'rule of law', but that is simply not true. It takes more to a rule of law than so many thousands of pages written by lawyers. Not every text, not even every legal text, is capable of being law at all. Everyone who reflected on the nature of law in the past four thousand years has come to that conclusion. It is sufficient now to quote Sir Alfred Denning, as he then was, who gives the following introduction to the idea of the Rule of Law:

*'In order that right, and not might, should be the basis of society, the people must be under the rule of law, and there are four fundamental requisites which the law must fulfil:*

*(1) it must be certain so that the people may act safe upon it;*

*(2) it must be just so that they will approve of its being enforced;*

*(3) it must be readily ascertainable, so that they may know what their rights and duties are;*

*(4) it must be enforced by independent and upright judges in whom the people have confidence.'* Sir Alfred Denning. The Changing law. London, 1953, p.p. 3-4.

So-called EU law does not begin to satisfy any of these requirements. Indeed, on these criteria, it is the very opposite of law. It is not in any sense certain, for it changes every day. It is not in any sense just, or approved by the people, for the people are never even given a chance to approve or disapprove.

It is not in any sense ascertainable because, not to put too fine a point on it, it consists of so many thousands of pages of pseudo-legal gibberish which even lawyers do not understand. And the EU judges are neither independent nor upright. One only has to read one random judgement of the European Court of Justice to see it is a purely political court.

One may be tempted to conclude that it is the rule of lawyers instead of the rule of law - lawyers who govern us by giving orders to each other in their own secret language, which no mortal can decode. Such a picture strikes the imagination; but it actually misses the point. Their pseudo-legal language is not so much a code as a smokescreen; in most cases, it conceals not the meaning of the law, but the lack of it. There is hardly any law behind it, good or bad. After all, if you need to imitate the rule of law where there is no law, perhaps the only way to do that is by using sophisticated legal language. The point about the 'new legal order' is not that it is new, not even that it is worse than the old, but that it is not there.

In truth, the EU is, and always was, an ideological project. It is not there to safeguard such liberty and property as its subjects have; it is there to build a new political order. It is a new order to be governed by an ideology; and this always means there is no place for the law as understood under the English system. By their very nature, law and ideology are direct opposites.

The law is all about enforcing clear rules; an ideology is all about pursuing vague ideals. The law is naturally static; an ideology is naturally dynamic. An ideology is always a legend, a dream; it explains itself in metaphors; it strives to change the world and boldly challenges the dull reality. The whole object of law, by contrast, is to be as clear and precise as possible. The law has to be realistic, take due account of the imperfections of the world, and express itself in plain language. Consequently, one simply cannot write an ideology into the law – no more than the medieval scholasts could calculate exactly how many angels can dance together on the point of the same needle.

One would reasonably expect the EU law (if it were law), with its hierarchical structure, to be simpler than the English common law with its lines of authority going back into centuries. With the English law, one would need a lot of research and analysis to identify the key principles and to filter out accidental or temporary things. With the

EU law, nothing (one would expect) is easier: you just open the EU Treaty and the first chapter will give you the key principles in a neat form. Yet, if you do open it, you find a forest of enthusiastic political slogans, but no legal principles at all.

You learn, first of all, that "the Treaty marks a new stage in the process of creating an ever closer union among the peoples of Europe, in which decisions are taken as openly as possible and as closely as possible to the citizen". Praises are sung to human dignity, freedom, democracy, equality, rule of law and "human rights, including the rights of persons belonging to minorities". We learn that "pluralism, non-discrimination, tolerance, justice, solidarity and equality between women and men" must certainly "prevail".

In the next article, the EU vows to promote peace and well-being of the people; to be an "area of freedom, security and justice", to "work for the sustainable development of Europe based on balanced economic growth and price stability, a highly competitive social market economy, aiming at full employment and social progress, and a high level of protection and improvement of the quality of the environment", to "combat social exclusion and discrimination", to "promote social justice and protection, equality between women and men, solidarity between generations and protection of the rights of the child".

In the next round the EU swears to contribute to "sustainable development of the Earth, solidarity and mutual respect among peoples, free and fair trade, eradication of poverty and the protection of human rights, in particular the rights of the child, as well as to the strict observance and the development of international law, including respect for the principles of the United Nations Charter". And so on and so forth, page after page, after page.

All this claptrap may or may not have some meaning in the political newspeak of this particular Utopia, but this is certainly not a legal language. Lawyers, with all their faults and follies, do not speak it and do not understand it.

Nor is it a harmless ritual preamble to a real, meaningful law. All EU law is made with reference to these central slogans, and must be interpreted on their basis. For example, the European Arrest Warrant comes under the headings of 'common area of freedom, security, and justice', 'loyal cooperation', 'mutual trust' and 'mutual recognition'.

Let us examine a case in the real world for a moment. Suppose there is a legally doubtful European Arrest Warrant for a young British citizen on a charge of manslaughter in Greece. Suppose there is strong evidence that the Greek police have beaten witnesses into giving false statements; and if they get the suspect in their custody they are equally likely to mistreat or torture him into giving a false confession.

The Greek warrant comes before a British court, and the judgement goes along the following lines: Of course, usually this kind of things is seen as abuse; but we are under an obligation to interpret the law in conformity with the purposes of the EU law. The EU Framework Decision on European Arrest Warrant states its purpose is to create a 'common area of freedom, security and justice', and that it is based on mutual trust and loyal cooperation. Therefore, we have to trust the Greek police and cooperate with them. It is obvious that if we refuse to surrender suspects, this does not help to create a common area of freedom etc., or, for this matter, the ever closer union between the peoples of Europe. As the Greek Public Prosecutors office said:

> *"The absence of even an investigation before extradition into what has been shown by the defendant here may seem uncomfortable; the consequences of the Framework Decision may be a matter for legitimate debate and concern. But we have no doubt but that the common area for judicial decisions in criminal matters means that the judicial systems of the countries of the European Union must be regarded as capable of providing sufficient minimum safeguards for a fair trial in a civilised country, including provisions for the exclusion of evidence obtained by coercion."* Symeou v Public Prosecutor's Office at the Court of Appeals, Patras, Greece [2009] EWHC 897 (Admin).

This example is a summary of the case of a young London man Andrew Symeou. He was extradited under an EAW to Greece in 2009. He was held in the vile Korydallos prison for 11 months, mistreated and abused, before being released to be held on bail in

Athens for a further year. When his case eventually came before the Greek court he was found innocent. The evidence, or rather lack of it, against him should have been taken into account by the English court considering the EAW and his extradition should have been refused, but this was not an option for the court under the EAW procedure. A young man's life was devastated, and his family were financially drained in paying for his defence. But what is a young man's fate when weighed in the balance against a noble ideal?

If the courts have to follow the 'EU law', such results are inevitable, for the entire EU law is dominated by such political slogans. The courts have to answer legal questions on the basis of whether their decision would bring us closer to the European dream, sustainable development of the planet, greatest happiness of the greatest number, and all other angels dancing on the point of this needle. This is the end of the rule of law.

### EUROPEAN ARREST WARRANT AND HABEAS CORPUS

It is quite ironic that Mr. Symeou was sent to Greece by the same Lord Justice Laws who, several years before, talked in Metric Martyrs about "the event which no doubt would never happen in the real world, that a European measure was seen to be repugnant to a fundamental or constitutional right guaranteed by the law of England". On that occasion, the existence of the European Arrest Warrants was certainly very far from his mind – or he would never have said "never".

Habeas Corpus Act 1679 is still in force, and it is certainly a 'constitutional statute'. In section XI, it reads:

And for preventing illegall Imprisonments in Prisons beyond the Seas noe Subject of this Realme that now is or hereafter shall be an Inhabitant of Resiant of this Kingdome of England Dominion of Wales or Towne of Berwicke upon Tweede shall or may be sent Prisoner into Scotland Ireland Jersey Gaurnsey Tangeir or into any Parts Garrisons Islands or Places beyond the Seas which are or at any time hereafter shall be within or without the Dominions of His

Majestie His Heires or Successors and that every such Imprisonment is hereby enacted and adjudged to be illegall

Habeas Corpus Act has never been repealed. As a constitutional statute, it cannot be simply overridden by a later Act of Parliament. Here we have a constitutional right which the EU has no power to abrogate. Yet, thousands of people are being sent beyond the seas on European Arrest Warrants every year.

However, Habeas Corpus has been unlawfully set aside in relation to European Arrest Warrant cases. This is illustrated in the case of a Mr Hilali residing in Britain. Mr Hilali may not be a person deserving much sympathy, but as we have noted already, the law is often defined in relation to such cases. Hilali was wanted by the Spanish authorities on vague accusations related to terrorism. The European Arrest Warrant made only one accusation against him, that phone calls were made by him to a Mr Yarkas, who was charged with terrorism.

While Mr Hilali fought a desperate battle to avoid extradition on legal technicalities, Mr Yarkas was cleared of the terrorist charges by the Spanish court. Hilali then applied for a writ of Habeas Corpus citing unlawful imprisonment. The High Court found that the Spanish trial had destroyed any grounds for the accusations against Hilali and granted the writ.The Spanish court then appealed to the House of Lords. The Lords ruled that the Extradition Act (2003) deprived the suspect of his right to Habeas Corpus, and therefore he had to be extradited, even in these circumstances.

The highest court in the land had set aside Habeas Corpus, although it has never been expressly repealed. So either Mr Justice Laws is right and Constitutional Acts cannot be impliedly repealed, and the Lords are in breach of our Constitution, or he is wrong, and they are not. Either way it is another fine mess that membership of the European Union has gotten us into.

Furthermore, under the same section of Habeas Corpus Act, it is an offence of praemunire to "knowingly frame contrive write seale or countersigne any Warrant for such Committment Detainer or Transportation or shall soe committ detaine imprison or transport any person or persons contrary to this Act or be any wayes adviseing

*The Human Rights Act of 1998 was introduced by the government of Tony Blair. The Act makes it unlawful for any public body to act in a way which is incompatible with the Convention. It also requires UK judges to take account of decisions of the Strasbourg court when reaching decisions.*

aiding or assisting therein". This is the only form of praemunire which was not abolished in 1969. All the Law Commission did was to soften the punishment. It used to be outlawry, forfeiture of all property and goods, and life imprisonment. Now it is simply life imprisonment.

## HUMAN RIGHTS ACT 1998

The malicious intent of those who sold England's Crown and liberty to Brussels can be proven beyond reasonable doubt before any jury. By contrast, our road to Strasbourg was paved with good intentions. If the EU Constitutional Treaties are a brutal invasion into our sovereignty and democracy, the Human Rights Act is a much more interesting illustration of the present constitutional crisis.

It is not necessary to recite the examples of practical injustice it continues to cause - alas, we get new examples almost every day; but its fundamental flaws are deeper and subtler, and not nearly so obvious as with the 'EU law'. It was not for nothing that the issue caused a furious division between our top judges, many of whom quite sincerely think that the Human Rights Act strengthens the rule of law and checks the arbitrary power.

The problem is not that the human rights are a foreign idea. Paradoxically, the problem is precisely that the human rights are an English idea. The rights and liberties listed in the European Convention were among those protected by the common law long before most of Europe ever heard of them. For a number of centuries, while England enjoyed and developed those rights, Europe moved to where its own 'legal positivism' led her. It then required two world wars and a global Cold War for the common law nations to rescue her from there.

Having done that, we took a piece of paper, put down a short list of the most basic principles of the common law in simple words, and offered it to Europeans as a basic safeguard against repeating their former, should we say, eccentricities. This is what the European Convention of Human Rights is: a beginner's course in the Common Law. Making it the supreme law of this country, as the Human Rights Act does, more or less brings us several centuries back.

If the Russians or Turks or even the French, in their humility, insist on being judged by a British judge, this might be a good idea for them; but no Englishman in his right mind would prefer to be judged by a Russian, Romanian, Bulgarian or Turkish judge; not even if the law they apply is English in origin. It is not even so much a question of sovereignty or constitutional principle as a question of practical common sense.

To put Moldovan or Ukrainian judges on a par with the English ones is the sheer indulgence of political correctness. Nobody wants to denigrate other European nations, whose own achievements in their own particular fields are only to be admired. There are no useless nations in Europe; but there are two fields of human activity - if not only two - where England can teach a lesson to anyone who is interested but should really take no lessons herself: and those are Law and Government.

It is not even that we are several centuries ahead of them. Rather, it is about law and government that England violently disagreed with the rest of Europe for many centuries, and has now been proven right. Even now, some of these nations have not fully accepted democracy or the rule of law. It is a bit rich to ask us to accept their Strasbourg judgements on human rights.

Of course, accepting a jurisdiction of any foreign court such as Strasbourg is unconstitutional. It is a crime of praemunire; and there are good reasons why it should be so. Like the EU, it is a breach of sovereignty; like the EU, it is undermining the rule of law.

Many judges like the Human Rights Act, or at least used to like it; and out of pure motives, too. While the Parliament is legislating so frantically and so absurdly, they are desperate for some check on its 'elective dictatorship', some lex legum above and beyond arbitrary political legislation. So they cling to human rights – for that is a distant echo of the old common law and its great charters. What they fail to appreciate is just how distant it is; how much, after being copied from Magna Carta, those rights have been re-defined, simplified, and corrupted by Strasbourg.

It is true that the Human Rights Act takes considerable power away from politicians and gives it to the courts. This may seem to help protecting the rule of law; but in fact, it does not. Here, once again, people fall into the trap of analysing the English Constitution from the point of view of power, its checks, balances and separation; and that is a very misleading analysis.

The strength of common law courts is not in the amount of their 'power', but in the fact that they apply clear and precise law, and care nothing for everything else. Yet, taken out of their native soil, the human rights in Strasbourg have grown more and more like political declarations. They became flexible; they can be turned to the advantage of either side at the judge's pleasure, in a way Magna Carta could never be turned. Human rights became simply an excuse for arbitrary judges overruling arbitrary politicians. The law is neither here nor there.

As Lord Justice Shaw said in Scott v. Scott (1913) , "to remit the maintenance of constitutional right to the region of judicial discretion is to shift the foundations of freedom from rock to sand". This is what Human Rights Act has done.

### 'INDEPENDENT AND UPRIGHT'?

Moreover, the Courts of Law themselves are no longer the same as they used to be. Year after year, decade after decade, fewer and fewer cases are being decided at a trial by jury. More and more cases are heard behind closed doors. And worst of all, our judges and magistrates are no longer as 'independent and upright' as they once were.

For most of the 20th century, one of the persistent campaigns of the Left was for a 'politically balanced bench' and against the judiciary being predominantly 'white, male, Oxbridge', and therefore having a wrong kind of mindset. Successive Lord Chancellors resisted such demands until the position was taken by Lord Elwyn Jones of the Labour Government of 1970s. Lord Elwyn Jones shared the 'politically balanced bench' objective. The civil servant from the Lord Chancellor's Department who was then responsible for appointment of magistrates, Sir Thomas Skyrme, later wrote in his book The Changing Image of the Magistracy:

Lord Elwyn Jones gave a great deal of thought to solving this problem and he enlisted the help of the Labour Party and the TUC. Both General Secretaries, Len Murray and Ron Hayward, agreed to assist in finding suitable candidates through their respective organisations while accepting the Lord Chancellor's insistence that the choice must turn on suitability for the job and not on the candidates' service to the party or union. The results were disappointing. By the time the recruiting scheme passed to regional and local level the emphasis on judicial quality was forgotten and was replaced by the old bogey of swamping benches with leading Labour and union supporters (in total disregard of the Chancellor's warning that these tactics were bound to be detrimental to the party and union image). Some branch organisations demanded the right to nominate members of Advisory Committees and even to have their own nominees appointed to the bench without question. In many areas the Lord Chancellor's well-conceived plan was totally misconstrued and merely served to generate a militant reaction.

Unfortunately, all other sources on the history of the magistracy in the UK – including Skyrme's own fundamental 1470 pages long History of the Justices of the Peace, published 11 years later - remain silent on this secretive 'reform' of Lord Elwyn Jones. It remains pretty much shrouded in mystery. The archival documents from the Lord Chancellor's Department which might shed some light on it remain classified to this day.

Generally, Sir Thomas Skyrme's writings follow the classic discreet style of the civil service, so the above, coming from him, amounts to very strong criticism. It would be a legitimate inference that Lord Elwyn Jones's experiment ended in a disaster of large numbers of communists and Trotskyites aggressively capturing the seats of magistrates.

The name of Ron Hayward, mentioned in the above passage, is particularly worrying in the light of later-day revelations. It has emerged from the Soviet archives that Hayward worked closely together, albeit secretly, not only with the Communist Party of Great Britain, but also with KGB agents. Indeed, he was a Soviet agent of influence in all but name.   See Pavel Stroilov, Reaching through the Iron Curtain - The Spectator, 7 November 2009.

He was also one of the fiercest far-Left fighters in the 'civil war'; he had little regard not only for the English Constitution, but even for the Labour Party's own constitution. For instance, in 1979, Hayward made an infamous attack on the Party leadership at a conference, which was seen as grossly improper for any paid servant of the Party, not to mention such a high-ranking one as the General Secretary. Sir Gerald Kaufman described him to one of the co-authors as the worst General Secretary he could remember, 'very lazy and inefficient', who put the factional struggle above the duty of his office. There is hardly much doubt that, when asked for assistance in recruiting suitable left-wing magistrates, Hayward was unlikely to miss the chance to use this new kind of influence to promote the factional interest.

After the New Labour's return to power in 1990s, the attack on the judiciary renewed. It was impossible to remove the old judges, but it

*Olvier Cromwell's attempt to rule without a monarch proved to be disastrous from a constitutional point of view and shows the folly of seeking to change dramatically the constitution of England without thinking through the changes.*

is rumoured among legal professionals that Tony Blair approximately doubled the overall size of the judiciary, and the difference between the old judges and new ones was easily noticeable. While traditionally judges are only appointed after a long and successful career as a barrister, the new generation judges were all rather young, and would therefore remain on the bench for many decades. One eminent barrister told us on the condition of anonymity: "It happened almost overnight across the country, as simple as this: you come to the same court, but suddenly you have a young judge you have never seen or heard of before, making decisions you would have never expected."

### WE LIVE IN AN ILLEGALLY CONSTITUTED STATE

In retrospect, the destruction of our Constitution looks like an awfully clever plot. The Constitution, it would seem, was protected against everything. How can you subvert the Constitution in a country where the courts can review the legality of every step taken by the government? Yet, there was one narrow loophole. International treaties are not subject to judicial review. They are supposed to be about war, peace, and other foreign affairs which have nothing to do with law, and are therefore outside the jurisdiction of the courts. So, they crawled through this loophole – they made international treaties about constitutional law of this country.

Against this, however, there were constitutional safeguards, too. The government is free to make treaties precisely because the treaties, in themselves, never affect the law of the land. All these constitutional changes were still floating somewhere in the high seas of international relations. How could you import them into the country where every step of every public authority is subject to judicial review?

Here, they crawled through another loophole. An unconstitutional decision by any public authority would have been quashed by the courts; an unconstitutional judgement of a lower court would have been quashed by a higher court. But the highest court of all, the Parliament, is the only authority in the country whose decisions cannot be "impeached or questioned in any court or place out of Parliament". So they did it by Acts of Parliament.

But how can you make an elected Parliament vote for an unconstitutional Act? Is not Parliament democratically accountable to the voters? Yes; but the voters first have to know what their elected representatives are doing. They can only know this from the media; so you only need to prevent the media from reporting it. Surely you cannot stop the media reporting no lesser a matter than a coup d'état against the Constitution?

You can: by its very nature, the media tends to report simple and interesting things; and you cannot blame them, because that is what the public wants to see, hear and read. So, what you need to do is to make your coup d'état very complicated and very boring. That has been achieved by covering it up with thousands of pages of legalistic gibberish. It does not matter that the whole thing has very little to do with the law; what matters is that the legal language scares all the journalists away. There is a level of complexity and boredom beyond which anything becomes immune from media reports; and highly legalistic nonsense is what you need.

By now, all decisions of any significance are taken in Brussels; and yet, the press hardly ever reports them. Instead, they report the everlasting performance in Westminster village, which is of little consequence to the country. The Westminster actors put all their effort into being reported in the media, and therefore are careful to keep the performance simple and interesting; whereas Brussels decision-makers put all their effort into not being reported in the media, so they cover everything they do with countless pages of legal nonsense.

So the traitors have successfully crawled through this maze of loopholes and technicalities, avoiding all the safeguards of law on one hand and all the safeguards of democracy on the other. Everybody knows what they have done is illegal. And yet, no court in England has jurisdiction to judge them; not even the great democratic court of public opinion. Now we know, but it is too late to stop them.

This brings us back to where we started. The law is not a command of the sovereign. The law is not a command of the Parliament. The law is not a command of the judge. The law has been developed since time immemorial; before any sovereigns, parliaments and judges, and has created them all. And even if all parliaments and courts have become lawless, the law is still there. What those people have done is illegal; and this means that, in the eyes of the law, it is void. Even if the EU could survive for a thousand years, this usurpation of sovereignty would remain as unlawful a thousand years hence as it is now.

Yet, as things stand now, our Constitution and Sovereignty have become legal fictions, while the EU usurpation remains a de facto political reality. As a matter of law, our Constitution remains immutable; but as a matter of fact, we live in an illegally constituted state.

Things like this have happened before. King John also had lawyers, and they also argued that everything he said was law and everything the Barons said was out-of-date medieval rubbish. Cardinal Wolsey, Charles I, Cromwell, James II – they all had their own lawyers who persuasively argued that the old common law was obsolete. There were many usurpations in our history, but the Constitution has always won. For, there is no wrong without a remedy.

At an earlier page, we considered the theory that the Parliament can legally do anything, and discovered the Parliament was in no way special in that. The Queen, the courts, the subjects, almost anybody can legally do almost anything, but only in very special circumstances. One might wonder why the Constitution did not place any absolute checks on these powers.

The answer is that these powers are there in case they are needed. It is, if you like, a constitutional nuclear deterrent. If the Crown begins to abuse its unlimited powers, then (and only then) the Parliament has its own unlimited powers to check it. If the Parliament begins to abuse its unlimited powers, then (and only then) the courts have their own unlimited powers to shoot every act of such a Parliament to the ground. And if all of them support the usurpation, this is asking for a lawful rebellion.

This is the rule of law, so whoever is genuinely on the side of the law is always right. By definition, it is lawful to stop a crime, a treason, an usurpation. It is lawful for anyone – a Parliament or a

Court, the Queen, or a subject. The common law lives and rules - so long as there is anyone at all who is prepared to stand and defend it.

*King James II ruled from 1685 to 1688. He was overthrown by Parliament after he attempted to introduce to England a form of absolutist monarchical rule that was gaining ground on the Continent. The constitutional settlement agreed by Parliament and James's successors, William and Mary, endured until 1973.*

# PART III. RESTORATION

## THE LEGAL SOLUTION

Today, the *de facto* government of this country is in Brussels, so our grievances against the EU cover every aspect of national life. It has blighted our economy; it has swamped the country with millions of immigrants; it has exposed British subjects to arbitrary arrests on European warrants and to unfair trials in places like Greece and Hungary. These things were not evident from the outset, even if they were foreseeable; but from the very beginning, our membership in the EEC was illegal. In a country living under the rule of law one would expect our courts of law to say so. Yet they did not.

Whenever we see the law broken, it is our natural instinct to go to court; so it is rather frustrating that they refuse to do anything about the most massive and wide-ranging breach of law of our times. Partly, this is due to the quiet coup of New Labour, who appointed a whole new generation of judges with question marks over their political impartiality.

Partly, this is due to the old folly of seeking the help of today's enemy in fighting against yesterday's one. Some in the older generation of judges still believe that the biggest threat to the rule of law comes from the 'omnipotence' of Parliament, and cling to every limitation of it - and 'EU law' is very much of a limitation. What they fail to see is that it is an even greater limitation on the rule of law itself.

All this said, the Courts have their own constitutional limitations. Looking now at these old judgements – Blackburn v Attorney-General, McWhirter v Attorney-General, etc. – it is hard to blame the judges. The Courts cannot usurp the Royal Prerogative to make or to denounce international treaties. This is a power which the Constitution assigns to the Crown, not to the Courts. Nor can they usurp the Parliament's power to enact or repeal statutes. The judges have always taken the view that they should enforce the statute law as it is made by Parliament. Whether a statute is good or bad is a political debate, which belongs to Parliament and other institutions of political democracy.

Generally speaking, these are sound constitutional principles. Usurpations of power by unelected judges and lawyers are no better than any other usurpations. Yet, while such a separation of powers is a sound constitutional safeguard in the ordinary course of events, it made the courts powerless to protect the Constitution when such protection was so desperately needed. At the time these demarcation lines were drawn, nobody envisaged that the Parliament and the Crown alike would fall under control of political forces set on systematic destruction of the English Constitution. It was assumed that any such government would be ousted by democratic means without any need for judicial interference. It would be Parliament itself which restores the Constitution, as it did in 1628 or in 1689.

Yet, if this does not happen, the Courts do have power to 'control' the statutes. At the very least, they can insist on interpreting them very narrowly.

It does happen that, for constitutional reasons, the courts find they have to stretch the words of a statute as meaning less than what it says. There are limits to this, and the courts are generally reluctant to take this slippery slope if they can help it. Yet, they have this power; and as the threat to the rule of law grows more and more serious, the extraordinary threat warrants extraordinary decisions by the courts. After all, it did happen before in our history that the political government tried to take the courts under control. Yet, it is simply unnatural for our courts to be enemies of the common law. The common law shall be defending itself through the courts. Yet, it is also in the nature of the common law that it works very slowly.

Probably our strongest point is that the destruction of the Constitution is treason; at least the government has never found any legal answer to that. Albert Burgess, the author of the brilliant Layman's Guide to English Constitution, is now running a campaign of reporting this treason to the police officers and other authorities all over the country. The strength of this approach is that under the law, any official why suppresses such a report becomes guilty of a criminal offence himself.

Yet, the official prosecutors do suppress such reports now and again. The authors understand that the Attorney-General's office even deliberately intervened to stop the prosecution of Douglas Hurd and Francis Maude for signing the Maastricht Treaty, initiated in 1993 by Norris McWhirter and Rodney Atkinson. The Attorney General, in his wisdom, considered that the prosecution was 'not in the public interest'. The charges they submitted to the court against the Government Ministers are long and comprehensive. These are given in detail under Appendix I at the back of this book.

## APPEAL TO THE SOVEREIGN

If the Courts have no jurisdiction to 'impeach or question' even unconstitutional actions of the Parliament, this still does not mean that the design of our Constitution includes no safeguards against them. The Bill of Rights reads: "proceedings in Parliament ought not to be impeached or questioned in any court or place out of Parliament". There is no wrong without a remedy; so all this means is that the remedy must be found within Parliament. It must come from either House or from the Queen. And indeed, all three are duty-bound to uphold the Constitution against all the odds.

Every MP and every peer have sworn allegiance to the Queen. And the Queen is bound by the Coronation Oath "to govern the Peoples of the United Kingdom of Great Britain and Northern Ireland, Canada, Australia, New Zealand, the Union of South Africa, Pakistan, and Ceylon, and of your Possessions and the other Territories to any of them belonging or pertaining, according to their respective laws and customs"; and the Accession Declaration: "I, A. B., do solemnly and sincerely in the presence of God profess, testify, and declare that I am a faithful Protestant, and that I will, according to the true intent of the enactments which secure the Protestant succession to the Throne of my Realm, uphold and maintain the said enactments to the best of my powers according to law."

Indeed, the monarch has always been considered "the Guardian of the Constitution". In this one role, exceptionally, Her Majesty has a right and a duty to interfere in politics. She can if necessary: overrule Ministers; withhold Royal Assent to Acts of Parliament; and reject advice from her Ministers.. Her Majesty's primary duty of safeguarding the Constitution overrides any other rules or duties.

Likewise, neither Lords nor Commons, while in general their decisions cannot be fettered by any rules, still cannot lawfully do anything against the Constitution. For they are bound by their oath of loyalty to the Queen, and loyalty to the Queen cannot be separated from the loyalty to the Constitution.

Alas, today the medieval legal fiction about 'evil counsellors' imprisoning the monarch has turned into an ugly and concrete reality. There is, perhaps, simply nobody around the Queen to advise Her Majesty what her constitutional duty is, and take responsibility for advising her of the extraordinary steps she is now obliged to take to protect the Constitution. Our Queen is now in captivity of traitors, quislings and cowards, and we are left without the protection which the law of this country provides in her royal person.

As loyal subjects, we still can and should appeal to the Queen to do her duty even in that desperate situation. But ultimately, the most realistic solution is also the most obvious one. It is the English democracy that can and will save itself. Our Queen needs us. She needs someone who can give her a proper constitutional advice, and the best constitutional position to give it is as leaders of parliamentary majority.

## DEMOCRATIC SOLUTION

One might expect that, since such a mess has been made out of the Constitution, it would take a great statesman of genius to find a way out. Oddly enough in fact everybody knows the way out. The whole country knows what to do about it; much more surprisingly, the whole Cabinet knows what to do. In their electoral manifestos, they have solemnly promised to do all the right things. The only problem is that they lied.

The Tories, Lib Dems, and Labour have all promised to hold a referendum on the Lisbon Treaty. All three knew what its results would be: a No vote that would halt the next stage of European integration. This is why all three parties had no intention of keeping their promises.

The only referendum ever held on the EU in Britain was in 1975. It is a common misconception that is was about Britain's entry into the European Economic Community (Common Market). In fact Britain joined in 1973 and the question was posed was:

Do you think the United Kingdom should stay in the European Community (the Common Market)?

The answer of the British electorate was 67.5% in favour with 32.5% against. The referendum campaign was a travesty of fairness and democracy. The BBC flagrantly broke its obligations under the Royal Charter to provide impartial political reporting in order to work for a Yes vote. The USA's Central Intelligence Agency (CIA) pumped in money to the Yes campaign as it suited US foreign policy at the time to keep Britain in the EEC. It is estimated that the Yes campaign had as much as twenty times more money to spend as the No campaign. By means of money, lies and foreign intervention, the British people were robbed of their birth-right.

If a referendum is held in the future then the only meaningful question would be for a simple In or Out choice of EU membership. This would have to be totally fair, with equal money, and exposure in the media, given to both sides of the argument.

Having left the EU (if not before) we need to repeal the Human Rights Act. The Tories promised to do that. They lied.

Moreover, we need a Great Repeal Act, a bonfire of unconstitutional and oppressive laws passed by the treasonous Parliaments over the past several decades. The Tories promised that. Once in office in 2010, they limited it to some cosmetic changes. They only repealed some of the most odious and oppressive laws against civil liberties; but if it was a Repeal Act, it was anything but 'great'. What great repeal is that, if it does not reach to the two most hated statutes – the European Communities Act and the Human Rights Act?

They did not even repeal the law on detention without charge for up to 42 days, which they had always rightly cited as a hideous example of the New Labour 'police state'. The New Labour is gone, but the police state is there to stay. Once in power, the Tories have found it perfectly convenient to keep it.

We need another declaratory and constitutional Act of Parliament along the same lines as the Petition of Rights or the Bill of Rights - confirming our ancient liberties which have "almost fallen into disuse, or become disputable". The Tories have promised us a new Bill of Rights to replace the European Convention.

I do not know, and I seriously doubt if anyone will ever know, whether they meant the same thing as we do here - for they have broken that promise before giving us any details of it. They no longer intend to pass a new Bill of Rights or, for that matter, to observe the existing one.

We should pass a new Constitutional Referendum Act which says that no constitutional changes can be made by Parliament without a free and fair referendum of the people; and for the Act to become law it must achieve a two thirds majority of the vote.

Politics in Westminster today is conducted in thoroughly dishonest terms. Nothing illustrates this better than the cancer at the heart of British politics: membership of the European Union. On being elected in 2010 and forming the Coalition Government the Tories talked about the big society and bringing the people into the government of the country.

In reality, they only did two things, both purely decorative. First, they passed a law whereby the Parliament cannot transfer any more powers to the EU without a referendum. This sounds good but the problem is that they have passed it too late to have any real effect. Almost all powers have already been transferred to the EU. To take care of what may be left, there is the 'self-amending' Lisbon Treaty, which allows to transfer powers without asking our Parliament - or the nation. The Tories promised a referendum on that treaty, too – in fact that gave a "Cast Iron Guarantee". They lied.

On gaining office the Foreign Secretary, William Hague, said that there could not be a referendum on Lisbon because it had already 'become EU law'. The Treaty was enacted into law by an Act of Parliament with Royal Assent – and could equally be repealed by an Act of the Parliament if that was the wish of the people. Mr Hague showed himself to be either entirely ignorant of how Parliament works, or totally subservient to the EU. Whatever he may be Mr Hague is not ignorant of his own business.

But we should not expect too much. After all, the Tories are only as good as their masters in Brussels. But we must not single out the Tories for blame. Their partners in crime the Labour and Liberal Democrat parties are equally guilty. They have all either been directly responsible for the criminal betrayal of Britain or aided and abetted the various acts depending on their position at any one time in the game of musical chairs in the Palace of Westminster.

There is a clear and simple solution to the issues outlined in this book. We need a patriotic government that will: unconditionally leave the European Union; reaffirm the laws and customs that are our democratic birth-right; and put in place constitutional safeguards to ensure that the most shameful period in English history cannot be repeated.

That will only happen when there is the political will to make it so.

# Appendix I

**Charges Laid by Norris McWhirter and Rodney Atkinson against Douglas Hurd and Francis Maude as signatories of the Treaty on European Union (Maastricht) 1992. The prosecution was blocked by an intervention of the Attorney General on the grounds that it was not in the public interest**

*It being an offence at Common Law (see Halsbury 4th edition vol. 11 at 818) for a person who knows that treason is being planned or committed, not to report. the same as soon as he can to a justice of the peace we hereby lay the following information.*

*Case 1:*
*Whereas it is an offence under Section 1 of the Treason Act 1795 "within the realm or without ... to devise ... constraint of the person of our sovereign ... his heirs or successors."*
*On 7th February 1992 the Rt. Hon. Douglas Richard Hurd, Secretary of State for Foreign and Commonwealth Affairs, King Charles Street, London SW1 and the Rt. Hon. The Hon. Francis Anthony Aylmer Maude at that date Financial Secretary to the Treasury, HM Treasury, Parliament Street, London SW1 did sign a Treaty of European Union at Maastricht in the Netherlands, according to Article 8 of which Her Majesty the Queen becomes a citizen of the European Union (confirmed by the Home Secretary in the House of Commons: Hansard 1st February 1993) therefore "subject to the duties imposed thereby", subject to being arraigned in her own Courts and being taxed under Article 192 of the integrated Treaty and thereby effectively deposed as the sovereign and placed in a position of suzerainty under the power of the "European Union".*
*Therefore the said Rt. Hon. Douglas Hurd and the said Rt. Hon. the Hon. Francis Maude are guilty of treason.*

*Case 2:*

*Whereas it is an offence under section 1 of the Treason Act 1795 to engage in actions "tending to the overthrow of the laws, government and happy constitution" of the United Kingdom ... etc.. Hurd and Maude.... etc.. did sign a Treaty of European Union ... according to Article 8 of which "every person holding the nationality of a member state shall be a citizen of the Union" and according to Article 8a of which such citizens "shall have the right to move and reside freely within the territory" of any member state and according to Article 8b of which such citizens shall have the right to vote and according to which "Declaration on nationality" in the Final Act "the question whether an individual possesses the nationality of a member state shall be settled solely by reference to the national law of the member state concerned."*

*And that therefore the British people and Parliament will have no right to determine the numbers or identity of non-British nationals to whom other European Union member states can give residence rights and voting rights in the United Kingdom.*

*And whereas according to the Act of Settlement 1700 S4 "The Laws of England are the birthright of the People".*

*And whereas Sir Robert. Megarry (Blackburn v Attorney General, Chancery Division 1983 Ch77, 89) has stated that*

*"And a matter of law the courts of England recognise Parliament as being omnipotent in all save the power to destroy its omnipotence."*

*Therefore the said Rt. Hon. Douglas Hurd and the said Rt. Hon. The Hon. Francis Maude are guilty of treason.*

*Case 3:*

*Whereas it is an offence under the Act of Settlement (1700) for any "person born out of the Kingdoms of England, Scotland or Ireland or the Dominions thereunto ... shall be capable to be ... a Member of either House of Parliament"*

*And whereas according to R v Thistlewood 1820 "to destroy the constitution of the country" is an act of treason.*

*And whereas the term "municipal" has been defined by the European Court of Justice in 1972 as meaning "national":*

*"... the treaty entails a definitive limitation of the sovereign rights of member states against which no provisions of municipal law whatever their nature, can be involved."*

*and similarly defined by Lord Justice Cumming Bruce giving the majority verdict in McCarthy v Smith 1979 ICR 785,798:*

*"If the terms of the Treaty (of Rome) are adjudged in Luxembourg to be inconsistent with the provisions of the Equal Pay Act 1970, European Law will prevail over that municipal legislation"*

*Hurd and Maude...etc.. did sign a Treaty.... etc.. according to Article 8b of which "Every citizen of the Union residing in a member state of which he is not a national shall have the right to vote and stand as a candidate at municipal elections in the Member State in which he resides."*

*Therefore the said Rt. Hon. Douglas Hurd and the said the Rt. Hon. Francis Maude are guilty of treason.*

*Case 4:*

*Whereas the United Kingdom of Great Britain and Northern Ireland is a monarchy in which Her Majesty Queen Elizabeth II is sovereign and Head of State and a democracy, whereby the people of that United Kingdom rule by delegating their authority for periods of up to 5 years to the Parliament and Government in London.*

*And whereas, according to the Act of Settlement 1700 S4 "The laws of England are the birthright of the people"*

*And whereas Sir Robert Megarry (Blackburn v Attorney General, Chancery Division 1983 Ch 77,89) has stated that*

*"As a matter of law the courts of England recognise Parliament as being omnipotent in all save the power to destroy its own omnipotence."*

*And whereas according to R v Thistlewood 1820 to "destroy the Constitution" is an act of treason.*

*.... Hurd and Maude...etc.. did sign a treaty...etc.. according to Article 8 of which the British people, without their consent have been made*

*the citizens of the European Union with duties towards the same and according to Article 192 of the integrated treaty the British people can be taxed directly by that European Union without further process in the Westminster Parliament and according to Article 171 of which the British State can be forced to pay a monetary penalty to the European Union.*

*Therefore the said Rt. Hon. Douglas Hurd and the said the Rt. Hon. Francis Maude are guilty of treason.*

*Case 5:*

*Whereas, in accordance with the Coronation Oath Act, Her Majesty Queen Elizabeth II swore at Her Coronation in 1953 that she would govern Her subjects "according to their laws".*

*And whereas it is an offence under Section 1 of the Treason Act 1795 "within the realm or without...to devise...constraint of the person of our sovereign...his heirs or successors"*

*Hurd and Maude.... etc.. did sign a Treaty.... etc.. which extended the powers of the European Commission, the European Court. of Justice and the European Parliament in the new "European Union" to make and enforce in the United Kingdom laws which do not originate in the Westminster Parliament. And that this loss of democratic rights was without the express consent of the British people.*

*And whereas, according to the Act of Settlement 1700 S4 "The Laws of England are the Birthright of the people"*

*And whereas Lord Justice Robert. Megarry (Blackburn v Attorney General, Chancery Division 1983 Ch 77,89) has stated that"As a matter of law the courts of England recognise Parliament as being omnipotent in all save the power to destroy its omnipotence."*

*Therefore the said Rt. Hon. Douglas Hurd and the said the Rt. Hon. Francis Maude are guilty of treason.*

*Case 6:*

*Whereas it was established in 1932 that "No Parliament may bind its successors" (Vauxhall Estates v Liverpool Corporation IKB 733)*

*And whereas according to R v Thistlewood 1820 to destroy the constitution is an act of treason.*

*Hurd and Maude etc.. ...did sign a Treaty...according to which Article Q of which the Maastricht Treaty "is concluded for an unlimited period" and from which there is no right of nor mechanism for secession.*

*Therefore the said Rt. Hon. Douglas Hurd and the said the Rt. Hon. Francis Maude are guilty of treason.*

*This is one of the more extraordinary aspects of the Maastricht Treaty since it provides a direct parallel with that other "Union", the American Union signed by the Southern, confederate states on the assumption that they could leave that Union whenever they wished. But they had omitted to ensure that both the right to and mechanism for withdrawal were included specifically in the Union declaration. As a result, the American President Abraham Lincoln (inaugural address 4th March 1861) justified war against the southern states by saying:*

*"No state upon its own mere motion can lawfully get out of the Union" It was this issue and not the question of slavery (for which Lincoln had expressed accommodation in his inaugural address) which caused the American Civil War in which 600,000 died. The northern states were engaged not on a moral crusade but on an imperialist adventure, using the industrial and military might of the North to conquer the largely rural, raw material producing South.*

*Although the European Union as yet possesses no significant armed forces, this is the ultimate intention and an embryo Franco German force has already been set up. The possible exit from this "Union" of Britain, the second biggest paymaster, with the richest coal, oil and fishing reserves in Europe and with the world's largest investments in the American economy might one day tempt this new breed of Eurofascist to use the logic of Abraham Lincoln.*

*Case 7:*

*Whereas it is established by a statute in force, the Magna Carta (Chapter 29) confirmed in 1297 and last reviewed at the passing of the Statute Law Repeals Act 1967 that:*

*"No freeman may be...disseised...of his liberties or free customs...nor will we not pass upon him but by the law of the land."*

*This most durable pillar of the constitution is destroyed by a "Treaty of European Union"...etc....which disseises all free men of their liberties and free customs under the law of this land by subjugating their Government to the extension of the powers of the European Commission, Court. and parliament (in which latter the United Kingdom members form a minority of 87 of 567 voting members). Under Article 192 of the integrated treaty our free men are open to be taxed without further process of the United Kingdom Parliament and according to the "Declaration on nationality" in the Final Act of the treaty the number and identity of non British nationals given residence and voting rights in the United Kingdom will not be determined by the British Government. And further that the treaty extends majority voting in the Council of Ministers thus permitting other states to determine laws which govern British people. Under Article 8 of the Treaty free men are required to become citizens of the European Union "subject to the duties imposed thereby."*

*And whereas according to R v Thistlewood 1820 "to destroy the constitution" is an act of treason.*

*Therefore the said Rt. Hon. Douglas Hurd and the said the Rt. Hon. Francis Maude are guilty of treason.*

# ABOUT THE AUTHORS

*Gerard Batten has been a UKIP Member of the European Parliament for London since 2004. He was a co-founder of the UK Independence Party in 1993, and has written on a wide range of political subjects. Before becoming an elected politician he worked in the real word for almost thirty years.*

*Pavel Stroilov is a Russian historian and political exile living in London. He has smuggled secret Soviet documents to the West and was granted political asylum in the UK. He holds a law degree from King's College London and takes special interest in constitutional law.*

# FIND THE PUBLISHERS ONLINE

Website - www.BretwaldaBooks.com
Twitter - @Bretwaldabooks
Facebook - Bretwalda Books
Blog - bretwaldabooks.blogspot.co.uk/